"Some books on worship deal with biblical principles, others with the believer's experience of singing. Still others try to combine these. But *With One Voice* is unique in the way it integrates these. It reaches deep into the history and theology of Scripture to show what it was like then to sing from the heart to God and how that experience can be ours today. In this volume, Kidd shows us 'why our relationship with God can be deepened through song.' This is a deeply moving book and an antidote to worship wars."

John Frame, professor of systematic theology and philosophy,
Reformed Theological Seminary

"Finally Reggie has put in print the doxological riches he has poured into his students over many years of faithful service as a seminary professor and skilled practitioner. My friend of three decades writes with credibility and creativity because he is a lead worshiper before he is a worship leader. Thank you, Reggie, for reminding us that Jesus is the center, song, means, and end of our most consuming and privileged calling—the worship of the living God."

Scotty Smith, senior pastor, Christ Community Church,
Franklin, Tennessee; author, *Objects of His Affection*

"Here we have a thorough biblical theology of song—but far more. Dr. Kidd provides pastors, church musicians, and culture watchers with an insightful study of the many diverse voices that converge as the body of Christ finds its 'heart language' for singing the truth of the gospel as we respond to our Singing Savior. From Bach's *Mass in B Minor* to U2, from the Gaithers to Caedmon's Call, from Anglican psalmody to the simplest of American folk hymns, from the sinner's lament to the exuberant praises of the redeemed, Kidd unfolds a vibrant, multi-colored tapestry of faith-building, life-shaping artistic expression. Like a docent at a fine museum, he explains the treasures from the archives, but also helps the reader to understand the message of today's innovators.

"*With One Voice* has helped me to understand more deeply that our songs of faith resonate most fully—most Christianly—when believing communities draw on the strengths of high culture, folk culture, and popular culture (Bach, Bubba, and the Blues Brothers). As I grow in intimacy with the Savior, I understand the joys and blessings of deferring to the needs and preferences of my brothers and sisters."

Carl Stam, director, Institute for Christian Worship,
The Southern Baptist Theological Seminary

"Having spent many years of my life in the Christian music field, I am keenly aware of the need for scriptural context and wisdom in both the making of music and in its engagement in worship. Dr. Kidd makes us a great gift in this insightful book. He calls us away from the self-centeredness of our petty worship wars and from the narcissistic preoccupations that seem to afflict so much of today's worship, and he calls us to higher ground, to be swept up into the eternal Song of the Lamb. And he helps show us how. The riches he mines in Psalm 22 are alone worth the price of admission. I cannot think of a more valuable book for worship leaders, praise team members, composers of worship songs, or indeed anyone wishing to become a more thoughtful, focused, and biblical worshiper."

Darrell A. Harris, chaplain, Institute for Worship Studies;
president emeritus, Star Song Records

"Here is a true theology of praise, a real doxology. It is beautifully written, touching both our lamentations and our aspirations. Reggie Kidd makes the point that it is none other than Christ himself who is the ultimate worship leader. In short, the ministry of song is most faithful when it is inspired by Christ, for he above all is a 'Singing Savior.'"

Hughes Oliphant Old, Erskine Theological Seminary

"I've waited for this book for so long. The church desperately needs it and the world desperately needs a church which understands this book. If you read one book on worship, this is the one you ought to read. It will speak to your mind and keep you from being superficial and silly; it will speak to your heart and keep you from being cold and shallow; and then it will find its way into your way of worship and your life so that the world will know Him. Read this book! You will thank me for recommending it to you."

Steven Brown, president, Key Life radio program; professor,
Reformed Theological Seminary

"Here's a book that will deepen not only your appreciation for music, but also your love of God. Drawing from often unnoticed scriptural themes and contemporary cultural expressions, the book celebrates God's active role in redeeming creation and lavishing on us the remarkable gift of song. For any of us who are tempted to worship *worship* itself, here is a compelling call to let our music-making point away from itself to the majesty, glory, and beauty of God."

John D. Witvliet, Calvin Institute of Christian Worship

"Sometimes scholars do an excellent job of keeping the heart out of their writing, even if they're writing about worship. Reggie Kidd blends heart and mind beautifully. Reggie makes me seriously consider history and theology, but he also brings me to the core of worship—my heart before God. This is a great book."

Cliff Young, Caedmon's Call

WITH
ONE
VOICE

Discovering Christ's Song in Our Worship

REGGIE M. KIDD

BakerBooks
Grand Rapids, Michigan

© 2005 by Reggie M. Kidd

Published by Baker Books
a division of Baker Publishing Group
P.O. Box 6287, Grand Rapids, MI 49516-6287
www.bakerbooks.com

Printed in the United States of America

Library of Congress Cataloging-in-Publication Data
Kidd, Reggie M.
  With one voice : discovering Christ's song in our worship / Reggie M. Kidd.
      p.   cm.
  Includes bibliographical references and index.
  ISBN 10: 0-8010-6591-7 (pbk.)
  ISBN 978-0-8010-6591-0 (pbk.)
  1. Music in churches. I. Title.
BV290.K53 2005
264'.2—dc22   2005016007

CONTENTS

FOREWORD

I am well aware that a foreword to a book is supposed to be about the content of the book. But I am constrained to introduce you to the person whose heart and imagination you will meet in this writing; this in itself will say all I need to say as a foreword to his book. I must put my first meeting with Reggie in context.

I started the Institute for Worship Studies in 1999 and grew its graduate program semester by semester. I was about one year away from the start of the fourth class in the series—a class on the sacraments and spiritual formation. I scheduled a trip to Orlando to see my longtime friend, Luder Whitlock, the president of Reformed Theological Seminary. I wanted to glean from the wisdom he had gained by presiding over a seminary for many years.

Early on in the conversation Luder said, "We've got a professor here who is interested in worship. His name is Reggie Kidd. Want to meet him?" "Yes, of course, I would," I answered.

Fortunately Reggie was on campus and we soon met. I had been looking for a year for the right professor to team up with Carla Waterman, the other professor in this course. I had run through a number of names in my mind, but in each case there was a block

for one reason or another. However, within a half-hour of meeting
Reggie I knew he was the man. And indeed he was. He has served
the Institute for Worship Studies with distinction.

How did I know so quickly? You will find out in reading this
book. What I saw in Reggie and what you will meet in these pages
is not a dry intellectual but a man pulsating with the song of God.
With One Voice is no abstract analysis of song; it is a hymn, a song
of praise to God that comes from the heart of the writer. And the
heart that comes forth will not point you to himself but to the one
man who is the ultimate hymn of the universe, Jesus Christ.

That is the kind of man I saw in our first meeting in Orlando;
that is the kind of man I've met in his faithful teaching at IWS;
that is the kind of man who will come to you through the pages
of this book—a man who will lead you into the chorus of the
heavens and bless your soul.

Thanks, Reggie, for a great writing that reaches into the mind,
warms the heart, and causes our lips to break forth in praise.

Robert E. Webber
Myers Professor of Ministry
Director of M.A. in Worship and Spirituality
Northern Seminary

Preface

I offer this book in loving memory of one of my teachers, Edmund P. Clowney (1917–2005), gentle warrior, gracious statesman, clever wordsmith, and ardent lover of the church. Clowney introduced me to the biblical notion of Jesus Christ as a Singing Savior. Not only have I been unable to escape the clutches of the concept myself, I cannot help but try to share with others Clowney's view that our worship on earth is a participation in a gorgeous liturgy that Jesus Christ himself leads from heaven. With this book I hope to advance Clowney's legacy by wooing new converts to his perspective.

My publisher has asked me: Whom is this book for? My singular, consistent, and unwavering answer: my students. My life is spent with pastors (aspiring and present), with worship leaders (also aspiring and present), and with various stripes of thoughtful Christians who want to worship more deeply and help others do so too. My students at Reformed Theological Seminary in Orlando have given me somebody to write for specifically. Their dilemmas, discoveries, queries, and "ahas" have been foremost in my thoughts as I've written. I thank all of them. Special thanks go to several who have given me penetrating observations based on material in this book: Mark Balthrop, Joshua Cottongim, Phil Mershon, and Greg Thompson. In addition, Rick Gilmartin put my documentation in order and sought out permission to quote from songs.

"Where there are friends there is wealth," said the Roman playwright Plautus. Count me filthy rich. As I've written this book, Steve Brown has cheered me on when I needed it and kicked me in the pants when I needed that. Joel Hunter, Vernon Rainwater, and Tim Tracey have been accountability partners and soulmates in worship for a decade and a half. Though seldom acknowledged, their fingerprints are all over this book. Mark Futato and Richard Pratt have generously shared insights from the Old Testament.

A special measure of friendship is the willingness to read a nearly complete manuscript and offer appreciative but critical feedback to an anxious and exhausted author. Carla Waterman, Emily Williams, John Frame, Darrell Harris, and Joel Hunter have shown such friendship. With their urgings to be bolder here and gentler there, each has made this a better book. They (along with Byron Williams) saved me from some bad gaffes as well.

If I have anything to offer about Christ's song in the church, it's because of churches who have taught me to hear it. During my college years, I worshiped at Westminster Chapel (now defunct) in Williamsburg, Virginia, where, with folk guitars and a flute and a violin, we played hymns and '60s-era contemporary praise songs. During seminary, I reveled in the preaching of James Montgomery Boice and the richness of Robert Elmore's classical organ playing at Tenth Presbyterian Church in Philadelphia. My first job out of seminary was with Spanish River Church in Boca Raton, Florida, where I saw a portrait of Christ as Worship Leader in the joyous abandon with which Larry Crabb led our Sunday night singing. In graduate school, the Chapel Hill Bible Church introduced me to the vibrant music of the Catholic folk mass movement. There, gifted and classically trained musicians showed the grace of Christ by offering humbler music for the sake of their congregation. During the first decade of my seminary teaching, Northland, A Church Distributed, in Longwood, Florida, immersed me in disciplined, professional, and theologically astute contemporary worship. Now, I'm grateful to my co-laborers at Orangewood Presbyterian Church in Maitland, Florida, where weekly we pursue together the mission of putting Christ at the center of our song.

Chad Allen, my intrepid editor with Baker Publishing Group, has shepherded this project masterfully. He saw this manuscript at too early a stage and rough a form and yet didn't flinch. I'm grateful for his tactful suggestions in shaping this book and encouraging me to tell Christ's story and my own as vividly as I can.

Nobody has done more to give this book its voice than my wife, Shari. Relentlessly and patiently, she has challenged me to be more courteous to my reader. More, she lives a bold life in union with Christ, and is from him to me a living epistle on how to know "the power of his resurrection and the fellowship of his sufferings." His song fills her life, and through her, mine.

One of the reasons, I suppose, that the Scriptures speak of the delight of parenthood, especially of fatherhood, under the image of one's "quiver being full," is that children are arrows we shoot into the future. My three sons were little squirts when I started this book but now are teenagers on the threshold of adulthood. Thanks to two of them for allowing their stories to be a part of the story I tell with this book. Thanks to all three of them for the passion with which they seek to follow Christ in their various interests, from Flannery O'Connor to string theory to the electric guitar to the double bass to percussion to classical Greek to baseball to tae kwan do to Japanese sword training. They are arrows their mother and I let off into the future; it is our prayer that Christ's and the church's rich legacy of song will help them and Christ-followers of their generation to add their voices to his.

1

"A Red Guitar, Three Chords, and the Truth"

Why We Sing

A theology that cannot be preached is not worth having," I once heard a preacher declare. I can't argue with that. Truth that can't be applied isn't worth bothering about. It's what was right about philosopher Søren Kierkegaard's claim that "truth is subjectivity"—the whole premise of Christianity is that to do us any good God's love had to come down from heaven, right here to where we live.

Here's a corollary to the preacher's quip: a theology that cannot be *sung* is not worth having either. Authentic Christian faith is not merely believed. Nor is it merely acted upon. It is sung—with utter joy sometimes, in uncontrollable tears sometimes, but it is sung. "Words and music did for me what solid, even rigorous, religious argument could never do, they introduced me to God, not belief in God, more an experiential sense of GOD"—that's the way Bono, lead singer of the band U2, puts it.[1]

What is it about singing that takes us beyond mere belief or behavior?

Think of singing as a language that allows us to embody our love for our Creator. Song is a means he has given us to communicate our deepest affections, to have our thoughts exquisitely shaped, and to have our spirits braced for the boldest of obediences. Through music, our God draws us deeper into a love affair with himself.

"Do you love me?" What a moment it is when Tevye sings these words to his wife, Golde, in *Fiddler on the Roof*. Their oldest daughter has turned her parents' world upside down by telling them she plans to marry a man of her choosing rather than theirs. Stunned at such world-shaking bravado, Tevye realizes he can no longer take anything for granted. He looks at his wife of twenty-five years as though she were a stranger. He has to know: Have we simply been acting the part? With his musical question, "Do you love me?" he acknowledges a profound reality: acts of love are important to a relationship, but no less vital is the embodiment of that love in words.

No, it's not enough that for twenty-five years Golde has cooked her husband's meals, washed his clothes, milked his cows, shared his bed, and given him children. To his poignant, "Then you love me?" Tevye needs to hear Golde's (superbly understated), "I suppose I do." The song that passes between them bears a sacramental message: behind the cooking and the milking and the birthing, there is after all something exotic and mysterious.

That's the way it is with God and us. The singing makes our covenant relationship more than a mere contract. It is a mysteriously romantic intimacy as well.

Love, to be love, requires "fleshing out," and just as we could speak of Jesus as being God's incarnate song of love to us, the love we have for God is made incarnate in our songs. Our songs are the way we bring ourselves to him. They're the way we answer his, "Do you love me?"

I will never forget the intimacy of a night God and I spent in my '63 Rambler on a roadside somewhere in rural—very rural—Virginia. My brave little car had broken down trying to get me home from college. Since we had limped pretty far off the interstate, there were no Holiday Inns in sight. My surroundings reminded me of the then current movie *Deliverance* (released 1972), about outsiders' misadventures in Southern backwoods. Even so, the only thing I could think to do was to stay in the car overnight. The road was dark and narrow, and headlights kept whizzing by. It was unsettling. Late into the night, my guitar and I explored psalms: "As a father pities his children, so the LORD pities those who fear him" (103:13 RSV) . . . "Whither shall I go from thy Spirit? Or whither shall I flee from thy presence?" (139:7 RSV). In the midst of the words—sung out into what Simon and Garfunkel had mistakenly called "darkness, my old friend"—God showed up. And I knew for myself what David meant when he praised God as One who was "enthroned on the praises of Israel."

Would God have been there without my songs that night? Of course. But his presence would have been lost on me. That's my point. Song shapes our love for him and makes us "there" to his "thereness." That's why he asks, "Do you love me?" Not because he doesn't know but because he delights in our pleasure in him.

The Bible: A Biography of Song in the Church

In the biblical history, ironically, music begins outside the covenantal line as God's gift to nonbelieving Jubal.[2] But song eventually comes to mark the most significant of moments in the relationship between Israel and Yahweh, Israel's redeeming Lord. In fact, over the course of Old Testament history, singing emerges as a sure gauge of Israel's relationship to the Lord and the progress of her redemption.

Yahweh parts the Red Sea and the children of Israel sing, play instruments, and dance. Just before Yahweh takes them across the River Jordan, lest they forget what is going on, Moses teaches the Israelites a song about who is waging the upcoming campaign of conquest. Singing gets built into the covenant relationship both as fortification for battle and as warning against faithlessness.[3]

The warrior-poet David is dubbed "Sweet Singer of Israel."[4] He becomes both musical soul-soother to his predecessor Saul and designer of the sound system for a temple to be built by his own son and successor Solomon. There is a grain of truth in novelist James Michener's notion that, before David, Israel's faith is more austere and less lyrical.[5] With David's songs, a God who is invisible shows the shape he can take in the human heart. The One whose story of redemption from sin seems abstract compared to the Baals' earthy guarantees of procreation and harvest becomes more accessible. It soon becomes apparent that Israel's whole faith venture will take on a new flavor in the way that David has bared his soul before God through his psalms. His songs become the impetus for a generations-long project: hymn writers and collectors embody Israel's story and emotional life in the book of Psalms.[6]

Once the Israelites build the temple, God's glory cloud shows up as though in answer to the people's chorus and orchestra. In war, Judah sends a choir before, or rather instead of, the army, singing, "Give thanks to the LORD, for His lovingkindness is everlasting!" Increasingly, the prophets of the Old Covenant point to a future in which a new and final exodus will call forth "a new song" of deliverance and victory. As a result, in the latter stages of Old Testament revelation, God himself claims to be the prime Singer, exulting in his joyful victory over his people's enemies and quieting them in his love.[7]

Singing continues in the New Testament. Mary's Magnificat sounds the overture of the New Song Symphony to the God who keeps covenant with his people and extends his mercy to the nations. Jesus maintains that while John the Baptist came to teach a dirge of judgment, by contrast he (Jesus) came to lead a dance of joy. Accordingly, the Gospel writers lace their teachings about who Jesus is with lines from Israel's songbook. On his way to his arrest, Jesus pauses to sing a hymn with his disciples.[8]

In the first of many trips to prison for telling of Jesus's death and resurrection, the apostle Paul sings hymns. Paul tells Christians to fill their time together with song. In fact, his letters are so laced with poetry, scholars are still trying to figure out whether he composed hymns himself or whether he was so filled with his churches' worship that their songs thrust their way into his writing.[9]

In the book of Revelation, the apostle John sees the worship that is going on in heaven. Accordingly, he challenges churches on the earth, struggling as they are with persecution from without and faithlessness from within, to take their bearings from heaven's worship, and especially from songs that trumpet the triumph of the Lion/Lamb (Revelation 5). In anticipation of the sweet resolution of a new heaven and a new earth, John climaxes his book with a fourfold "Hallelujah Chorus" in triple forte at the wedding feast of the Lamb (Rev. 21:1–2; 19:1–10).

For two millennia, Christians have sung their theology—from catacombs to dorm rooms, and from cathedrals to football stadiums. Every distinctive shape the faith takes finds its own musical voice. Ambrose's robust trinitarianism both created and was supported by the florid hymnody of the church of fourth-century Milan. Gregorian chant both bespoke a quest of a spiritual music for the church and announced the ascendancy of the medieval church. In the sixteenth century, Martin Luther trumpeted his newfound grace as much through broadsheets and hymns as through sermons and books. Along the way, preachers and song-sters have paired off, and sometimes the songsters have shaped the message as much as the preachers: John Calvin and Louis Bour-geois, John and Charles Wesley, Dwight Moody and Ira Sankey, Billy Graham and Cliff Barrows. The evangelical uprising that began right after World War II and persists into the beginning of the third millennium is characterized as much by its "praise and worship" as by anything else. When groups think about starting new churches, they are as anxious to establish their "sound" as they are their message.

God is in the process of reclaiming our lost planet, and we who know the Redeemer are at the center of the action. Singing suits the way things are. As a result, Christians have been irrepressible sing-ers from day one. If I believed that "all we are is dust in the wind," I, unlike the rock group Kansas, would have a hard time dressing the situation up with song. My motto would be, "Stuff happens, and then you die." If I believed that at the base of reality lay pure chance, I'd have to wave a butane lighter in salute of John Cage's "music" of random sound, instead of wishing the whole corpus could be torched. As it is, however, I believe that what J. R. R. Tolkien said is true: every fairy tale is a foreshadowing or an echo of the biblical drama—we were lost, and then we were found. Praise and thanks come unbidden to the surface of my being—and precisely in the unbiddenness of my singing lies its rightness.

A song will illustrate. One of my coworkers teases me: "I always know it's you coming down the hall, because I hear the music first." I can't imagine it's a pretty thing, but I am an incorrigible singer, hummer, and whistler. My neighbors must get irritated, because whenever I mow my grass I find myself singing—and you have to sing loudly to hear yourself over a lawnmower. When I mow, the one song that forces itself into my consciousness more than any other is this, a folk hymn written in the 1860s and added to in the 1950s:

My life goes on in endless song, above earth's lamentations.
I hear the real, though far-off hymn, that hails a new creation.
Above the tumult and the strife, I hear its music ringing.
It sounds an echo in my soul. How can I keep from singing?

When tyrants tremble, sick with fear, and hear their death-knell
    ringing,
When friends rejoice both far and near, how can I keep from
    singing?
In prison cell and dungeon vile our thoughts to them are winging.
When friends by shame are undefiled, how can I keep from
    singing?

What though my joys and comforts die, the Lord my Savior
    liveth.
And though the darkness round me close, songs in the night he
    giveth.
No storm can shake my inmost calm while to that Rock I'm
    clinging.
Since Christ is Lord of heaven and earth, how can I keep from
    singing?[10]

Composed in the middle of a most uncivil Civil War and re-
shaped during the Cold War and its attendant paranoia, this is a
hymn of courage in the face of tempest and darkness and tyrants.
Launched though it is from a wounded and lamenting earth, it
is nonetheless a song of hope in the Christ who lives. Despite
the tendency to blunt the song's theology in most performances
these days,[11] the original verses by Anne Warner are explicitly
Christian: "The Lord my Savior liveth . . . Since Christ is Lord of
heaven and earth . . . The peace of Christ makes fresh my heart."
Thus, when Noel Paul Stookey sings it, he tellingly sings of "the
new creation," recalling the apostle Paul's claim that Christ's work
has made old things yield to God's new creation. When my friends
at Northland Church decided to record the song they added a

chorus to articulate the song the singer can't help but sing: "Singing, glory, glory to the Lamb."[12]

My absolute favorite version of the song is Eva Cassidy's kicking "gospel" rendering.[13] She sang it while she was trying to fight off the malignant melanoma that would eventually take her life. Perhaps that's why she sings with an urgency most who take up this song don't have. I know that there are different kinds of "prison cells" and "dungeons vile," and that melanoma—which I too contracted—is one of them. I know therefore that the gift of a song in the night does keep the darkness back, if barely—"Dear God, do not let my children grow up without a father." And I know that a response of unbidden song rings true because, and only because, Christ is indeed Lord of heaven and earth. I hope this was Eva Cassidy's hope—it is mine, for though my cancer was found at a much earlier stage than hers and appears to have been treated successfully, I know that the "far-off hymn" isn't as far off as it was pre-cancer. I know in a way I didn't before that Christ's victory over the grave promises "new creation." More importantly, I know that in the worst of my fears I can't keep from singing; death and hell have been plundered.

This hymn is a parable of the entire history of song in the church. It explains why we are such a singing lot. My friend Richard Pratt wrote a book about biblical interpretation called *He Gave Us Stories*. I was tempted to title this book *He Gave Us Songs, Too*. For, from the very beginning, God has been orchestrating a grand drama, the reclamation of his lost creation—and in operatic fashion, he has used his people's singing to carry the story line.

The "Fifth Voice"

Barbershop quartet singers claim that when their voices blend just right, they hear a "fifth voice." That aural illusion created by harmonics is, I believe, a divine whisper of something that is absolutely true of our singing when we gather in worship. For the Bible says that in the church Jesus is singing hymns to the Father (Heb. 2:12) and that, in fact, he is our Worship Leader (Heb. 8:2, literally, "Liturgist"). It is important for us to sing so we can hear that "fifth voice."

I said earlier that we sing because song is a gift that connects us to God—when we sing our theology, we own it more personally. But it's not enough to say that our singing connects us to God—somehow, it connects *him* to *us* too. I also said that we sing because to do so fits reality—song is an appropriate, even an unavoidable, response to the Christian story line. But there's more: God has written his Son into the story line as lead Singer. It's as though we were the congregation in a cosmic call-and-response spiritual, where the Leader's voice lays out a line, and we the congregation sing it back. This means we sing so we can sing *with* Jesus.

The Bible has been called "the greatest story ever told." It could also be called "the greatest song ever sung." It's a song of a Warrior-King who is intent on winning back his beloved from her false suitors and exulting over her with loud singing (Zeph. 3:17). It's a song of a Son-King who wails, "My God, my God, why have you forsaken me?" as he goes into exile for his beloved-turned-harlot. It's a song of his rising to claim a purified bride and leading a *Jubilate Deo* to the Father of all (Heb. 2:12).

When Paul tells his churches to "let the word of Christ dwell . . . richly" among them by means of "psalms, hymns and spiritual songs" (Col. 3:16 NIV), he's inviting them to do more than use music as a "warm-up" to the sermon. The song is not ornamentation; it is participation in the very redemption of all creation. It plays its own role in God's showcasing his saving power before humans and angels (Eph. 3:10).

The singing Paul talks about is more than a duty. It's more than a warm-up. It's a sacred activity, by which God's life and ours interpenetrate. When we sing, we are not alone. We join a song our Savior is singing, and our singing is a sharing in his reclamation of our lost race.

I believe that much of the difficulty we face in the church stems from the fact that we think it's all about us—our tastes, our preferences, our principles. So we debate styles, genres, levels of participation, and levels of volume. When we factor in the other Singer as well—this Singing Savior—our conversations, I submit, will take on a different tone.

Music as Mission

To recapitulate, we need to sing our theology because song is a means by which we relate to God, because song makes sense given the Christian view of reality, and because our singing is a participation in the very song of God. Further, we need to sing for the sake of a world that has lost the ability even to dream that the Christian vision might be true.

Disbelief today is not a function of logic; it stems from a loss of imagination. When a college student is told by her professor that Matthew, Mark, Luke, and John cannot be read as literal truth anymore, it's not the supporting evidence he offers that does her in. Nobody has found Jesus's bones in a tomb. No scandalous news bulletin is "just in" on the apostles. It's the professor's imperious tone of voice—and the fact that when our student looks around the classroom she sees no hands raised in dissent. She doesn't know anybody whose life is governed by the Gospels. Her soul has been shaped entirely outside the reach of places or people of soulcraft, like churches or ministers. Arguably the chief icon-maker of her day, Walt Disney, taught her to "wish upon a star" but not to pray to a living God.[14] This is what theologian David Kelsey means when he says that faith is faltering because "plausibility structures" have decayed[15]: "authoritative community" has been in decline, and a culture of disbelief has taken over. The facts haven't changed. The things that make the Christian hope thinkable have changed.

As though to anticipate a day like ours, Paul wrote that the church is the "pillar and support of the truth" (1 Tim. 3:15 NASB). He meant that God's people, gathered in life, in belief, and in worship, are his "plausibility structure." God's people—loving one another, submitting to a common life, praising his name, and telling his story—are the case God makes to a watching world, both visible and invisible (see Eph. 3:10).

I believe that in our day it's as important to help people "see" from their inner being again as it is to rehearse evidence that "demands a verdict." Prove to a person who believes chance is king that a dead man came back to life, and you're likely to get a shrug: "Hey, anything can happen. So what?" Embody the faith in a living community, and the dead indeed rise.[16] Sometimes we simply need to tell our story and sing our song. As Bob Dylan put it:

> Many try to stop me, shake me up in my mind,
> Say, "Prove to me that He is Lord, show me a sign."
> What kind of sign they need when it all come from within,
> When what's lost has been found, what's to come has already been?[17]

In the face of the deconstruction of the Christian view of reality, the great cultural task of Christians is the reclamation of the imagination. This needs to be worked out across a broad front—from the way Christians conduct themselves in the marketplace and in politics to the way they educate the next generation and shape their churches. As vital as anything is the way they engage the arts: painting, sculpture, literature, poetry, cinema, dance, architecture, and, of course, music.

For many people today, music is as close to God as they ever get. "Music is the young person's religion," offers a local minister, explaining why his ministry rents a bar on Saturday nights and pumps out the tunes.[18] Once more, I like Bono's verbal craftsmanship: "Music is Worship; whether it's worship of women or their designer, the world or its destroyer, . . . whether the prayers are on fire with a dumb rage or dove-like desire . . . the smoke goes upwards . . . to God or something you replace God with . . . usually yourself."[19]

In such a world, it seems lame to admit, "All I got is a red guitar, three chords, and the truth. . . . All I got is a red guitar, the rest is up to you," as Bono ad-libbed to Dylan's "All Along the Watchtower."[20] But, really, as fractured and skeptical as our world is, and as inadequate as our song seems to be, it's enough that our "smoke goes upwards" to the God who is and ever shall be.

Music opens the imagination to the possibility that what we see is not all there is. Felix Mendelssohn composed no religious works until he encountered Bach's *Passion According to St. Matthew*—after that, his work was God-soaked. Our singing says clearly that all other loves are idolatries without love of God. And it's not just the world "out there" who needs to hear that song; Christians can be as imagination-challenged as anybody.

I went to graduate school to test my faith in the truthfulness of the Bible against nonbelieving scholarship. I am not foolish enough to think that my faith emerged intact because I am so smart. What sustained me was worship with my brothers and sisters. Invading my reading Monday through Friday were Sunday's worshiping faces and voices. The faces were points of accountability. The voices made the Christian vision imaginable. The songs we shared kept my spirit from wilting.

It was the gospel music wafting out onto the street from "a ramshackle building with a cross on top" that got writer Anne

Lamott to look inside. She joined in on the "glorious noise" long before she could even stand to listen to a sermon:

> Something inside me that was stiff and rotting would feel soft and tender. Somehow the singing wore down all the boundaries and distinctions that kept me so isolated. Sitting there, standing with them to sing, sometimes so shaky and sick that I felt like I might tip over, I felt bigger than myself, like I was being taken care of, tricked into coming back to life.[21]

Christian belief is necessarily sung because when we sing it we own it better, because we just can't help ourselves, because singing puts us in the company of the Savior himself, and because it's part of what "tricks" those he's still after into coming back to life.

In the following chapters, I hope to take us further into why our relationship with God can be deepened through song. In chapter 2, we will look at the book of Psalms—there is no better source for finding words to let us respond to who God is and what he does for and in us. All by itself, the Psalter is a concise telling of Israel's story: one long pilgrimage from suffering to glory—it's our story as well. In a most amazing way, each generation of believers finds its experience of God enhanced by these songs.

In chapter 3, we will look at David's life—for good reason he was called Israel's "Sweet Singer." He is the clearest example ever to emerge—in the Bible or since—of a person whose relationship with God was shaped by song. As composer, proto-guitarist, singer, and sponsor of the book of Psalms, he has much to teach us about clinging to God in hard times, celebrating the victories he gives us, and pursuing his presence always.

One of David's psalms, the 22nd, receives closer examination in chapter 4, and that for two reasons. First, in this recounting of a time when God miraculously delivered him from attack, there is a perfect crystallization of Israel's journey from shame to fame. And second, in this psalm we find that David pointed to another singer, One who would sing of the deeper shame of the cross and rise to the greater fame of his resurrection. Psalm 22 introduces us to our Singing Savior.

From there, in separate chapters (chapters 5 and 6), we will explore how Jesus Christ takes up both sides of Psalm 22: the lament of abandonment and the chant of victory. It is no small thing to know that in the deepest sadness I will ever know, One has come to take my side—he sings a blues deeper than I can imagine and comforts me in my most desperately lonely moments. And there is nothing better—nothing—than knowing that the risen Christ lives right now in heaven, singing over his people—singing over me—with love. We all need to know much, much more fully the pleasure of joining his song.

In the final chapters (chapters 7 through 10), we will look at the rich texture—the timbre—of the Singing Savior's voice. Psalm 22 anticipates Jesus singing in a "great assembly" that includes Jew and Gentile, rich and poor, those who have already died and those who have yet to be born. It is a breathtaking panorama. Because those voices give Jesus's voice its special tonal quality, we have reason to think about how we may honor his voice by valuing one another's.

2

The Psalms

God's Songs and Mine

If song is so important to our relationship with God, what exactly should we be singing? Is there some sort of official score from which we are supposed to sing? Or do we just wing it?

Fortunately, God doesn't make us try to figure everything out for ourselves. I'm not saying there's no room for improvisation—when Paul tells us to sing our faith he does talk about "hymns" (crafted, poetic explorations of the faith) and "spiritual songs" (songs of instruction or ad hoc exclamations).[1] But the first thing he mentions when he tells us to sing is "psalms," by which I believe he means the 150 "Songs of Zion" collected in the book of Psalms. The Psalms are tenured, and there's a good reason why: they're God's songs. They're there, as theologian Eugene Peterson observes, to shape our prayer life.[2] They're there to answer singer/songwriter David Crowder's cry:

I need words as wide as the sky,
I need a language large as this longing inside.
And I need a voice bigger than mine,
and I need a song to sing You that I've yet to find.[3]

The Psalter's Story Line

Sometimes the book of Psalms is called "Israel's hymnal." There may be some argument about whether it is technically correct to call the Psalter a hymnal. It is hard to imagine a worshiping community actually singing all the way through some of them. A number of the psalms may have been intended more for personal reflection and meditation than for corporate song. Still, the dominant feel of the book of Psalms is that it is a collection of songs for God's people—whether together or alone—to sing to and about their Creator, Preserver, and Redeemer.

Like every hymnal with which I am familiar, the book of Psalms is laid out with a specific design. When the Psalter received its final form, probably during the period of Ezra and Nehemiah, its editors divided it into five sections. "As Moses gave five books of laws to Israel, so David gave five Books of Psalms to Israel,"[4] says the *Midrash Tehillim*, before enumerating the "five books":

- Psalms 1–41 (Book One);
- Psalms 42–72 (Book Two);
- Psalms 73–89 (Book Three);
- Psalms 90–106 (Book Four); and
- Psalms 107–150 (Book Five).

The Psalter thus takes on the character of a mini-Torah, a complement to the five books of Moses. It's not that the Psalter rehashes the Pentateuch, as though, for instance, "Book One" of the Psalter covers the same ground as the book of Genesis. It's more that in their mirroring the shape of the Pentateuch, the Psalms transfigure for us the way we read God's instruction. God wants us to adorn his Word with music because he wants his Word to be a delight to us, not a drudgery.

The organization of the Psalter reminds us not only of the law of Moses but of a pilgrimage through which God is taking his people. The Psalter helps to tell the story of a journey from suffering to glory and from lament to praise.[5] One statistical detail tells the tale: in Books One through Three (Psalms 1–89), so-called "laments" outnumber "hymns" of praise by a little more than two-to-one, while in Books Four and Five (Psalms 90–150), the proportion is reversed, and actually amplified—here "hymns" of praise outnumber "laments" seven-to-three.[6]

A story line moves through the five books. It's history from God's perspective and our place in that story. The first book features psalms from a troubled David—these psalms recount the obstacles God overcame in lifting David to the throne (Psalms 3–41). The second book reminds us of the transfer of rule from David to Solomon, and it marks the high point in Israel's history (Psalms 42–72). The third, though, shows God's people crying out from the Babylonian captivity, clinging to the presence of God in the face of the failure of David's dynasty (Psalms 73–89). In the fourth book, a people who have returned to their land but who no longer have an earthly king remind themselves (and us) that even during the pilgrimage under Moses, long before there was a King David, God was already their King and will always be their King (Psalms 90–106). The fifth book returns to the promises made to David and refocuses the hopes that "a horn of David" will emerge, a "new song" of deliverance will break out, and all of creation will praise the Lord (Psalms 107–150).[7]

"A pilgrimage is a journey undertaken in the light of a story," writes Paul Elie.[8] And when we give ourselves, as countless Christians have done through the ages, to a careful and systematic reading—and, yes, singing—through the psalms, Israel's story becomes ours. For many of us, this is when our lives stop being mere wanderings and become a purposeful journey to someplace.[9]

While the organization of the Psalter points to the Torah and to Israel's story, its placement at the head of the major section of the Hebrew Scriptures known as "The Writings" reveals something about God himself. For centuries the Hebrew Scriptures have been known among Jewish people as "The Law, The Prophets, and the Writings." This is not by chance. I think of these as revealing God's mind, God's will, and God's heart. The Law (the five books of Moses) has to do with God's authority as King, the self-known Knower, Imparter, and Arbiter of all wisdom and truth. The Prophets (including both the oracles of the prophets themselves and the historical narratives) show God to be the Prime Mover in history. According to the prophetic view, God shapes history by his very Word; through the prophets, God calls all individuals and cultures to account.

The Writings—and especially the Psalms, which are the centerpiece of the Writings—show us the priestly side of God. In doing so, they bring integration to the whole of the Hebrew Scriptures' portrait of God. The Bible's God is one who loves, delights in, grieves over and with, listens to, fellowships with, possesses, and marries his people. The Psalms communicate the passion of the God of Sinai—the God of the Torah—to be near to his people, to indwell them. As well, these poets sing what the prophets preach: God is invading history with justice and for redemption.

I'd like to look at the first two psalms in particular, because they provide a lens through which this whole phenomenon is visible. But before we do so, there is one more thing we ought to note about the book of Psalms as a whole. The presence of a hymnal in the Bible tells us something about ourselves as well as about God. Not only do we have minds that need to be taught by the kinds of things we find in the Torah and wills that need to be shaped by the priorities of the Prophets; we also have affections that need to be captured by the poets of the Writings. Being who we are, we need more than mere answers to questions such as, "What exists and why?" We need a relationship—the songs become solace, even when we cannot discern clear answers to all our questions. Moreover, we need more than a road map of where our lives are going and what we're supposed to do en route. We need nourishment for our heaven-hungry souls. We need songs that bring what singer/songwriter Michael Card calls "joy in the journey."

Most scholars think that the first two psalms were placed purposefully as an introduction to the whole of the book of Psalms. Each provides a unique perspective on why all the "Songs of Zion" are so important. Psalm 1 casts the whole of life as a choice between staying close to the Lord and living, or separating from him and dying. Psalm 2 looks at the grand conflict at the root of human history and demands that we choose the right side. With every breath we take we play out unimaginably momentous decisions—and we need songs like those that make up the rest of the Psalter to help us stay close to God and to keep us from turning tail.

How God Goes Deep

"Blessed is the person . . . whose delight is in the law of the Lord, and who meditates in his law day and night"—that's how the book of Psalms greets us. Psalm 1 is essentially a call to meditate on the Word of God. More literally, the Hebrew word for "meditate" (hagah) is "mutter"—"read in an undertone," suggests Holladay's *Hebrew Lexicon*.[10]

Anyone who has experienced the sing-song reading of the Torah in a synagogue or has been in the presence of a Jewish person rocking back and forth while chanting Scripture knows that the lexicon's characterization falls short of the mark. "He who reads the Torah without chant, of him can it be said as it is written, 'the laws that I gave you were not good'"—so says the Mishnah's Rabbi Johanan. From this, musicologist Eric Werner infers that the rabbis believed, "to recite scripture without chant was considered a minor sacrilege."[11] The whole approach to God is at stake here. It's about engagement, not detachment. As Peterson observes, Isaiah uses the same Hebrew word "meditate" (*hagah*) for the sound a lion makes over its prey (Isa. 31:4): "A lion over its catch and a person over the torah act similarly. They purr and growl in pleasurable anticipation of taking in what will make them more themselves, strong, lithe, swift: 'I will run in the way of thy commandments when thou enlargest my understanding!' (Ps. 119:32)."[12]

Accordingly, the Psalter is full of physicality: texts are sung, hands are lifted, hands are clapped, knees are bowed, stairs are walked, instruments are played. The words are designed to become part of us, and they do that by our physical contact with them. We're supposed to chew on them, sing them, and play them so they can orient us to who God is and who we are in relation to him.

The first psalm compares this physical engagement with God's Word to our letting ourselves be firmly planted like trees near water. The image is ironic. Actually *God* becomes more deeply implanted in *us*, expanding us from the inside out. This is part of the base meaning of the word *torah*, coming as it does from a verb (*yarah*) that, in addition to meaning "to teach," can be used for "to shoot" an arrow.[13] "The word that hits its mark," says Peterson, "is *torah*."[14] It's less that we plant ourselves more deeply, and more that God shoots his life further into us, so that we become more God-filled—which is to say, more ourselves. God's darts, shot deep into us, make us more deeply alive. That is why when she sang the Christians' songs, Anne Lamott began to feel bigger than herself—what she felt was the beginning of life with God inside.

As an introduction to the Psalter as a whole, the first psalm places before us life's grand choice. We can become more and more like the God-scoffers and share their fate, eventual dissolution; or we can become more and more like the Lord, full and vibrantly alive, which makes us more genuinely ourselves. As the psalmist warns later, to "forget God" is to lose one's very selfhood:

> But to the wicked God says,
> "What right have you to tell of My statutes
> And to take My covenant in your mouth?
> For you hate discipline,
> And you cast My words behind you.
> When you see a thief, you are pleased with him,
> And you associate with adulterers.
> You let your mouth loose in evil
> And your tongue frames deceit.
> You sit and speak against your brother;
> You slander your own mother's son.
> These things you have done and I kept silence;
> You thought that I was just like you;
> I will reprove you and state the case in order before your eyes.
> Now consider this, you who forget God,
> Or I will tear you in pieces,
> and there will be none to deliver."
>
> Psalm 50:16–22 NASB

When people—and God's own people need the warning as much as anybody else—try to forget him, they eventually refashion him after their false likenesses: "You thought that I was just like you" (Ps. 50:21 NASB). The result is a tailspin of sexual misbehavior, dissembling, and invective, a deforming of personhood that the seventh, eighth, and ninth commandments are designed to protect us from. This is what happens when the Torah doesn't take root within. It's a dynamic that Paul, the psalm-inundated apostle, would describe centuries later and with deadly accuracy in Romans 1. Paul says that the root problem is a lack of thankfulness: "they did not honor [God] as God or give thanks" (Rom. 1:21). The antidote the Psalms offer is a posture of praise—praise that is verbalized and praise that is lived:

> [The one] who offers a sacrifice of thanksgiving honors Me;
> And to [the one] who orders his way aright
> I shall show the salvation of God.
>
> Psalm 50:23 NASB

God is after a convergence of his character and ours. The Psalms offer as a chief means of attaining this convergence: "Sit and soak. Chew on this." We are told to plant ourselves like a tree on the bank of a waterway, meditating on, absorbing the Word. The patterning of poetry and song are intended to press the Word into our being. Several psalms are composed around acrostics, designed to do one thing: make sure the song is remembered, make sure it is anchored in our soul.[15] The linkage of mnemonic device, poetic form, the act of singing, repetition—all these combine to help these psalms become resources of the spirit, springing to consciousness when we need them: during the terrors of the night, the tears of the sickbed, the desolation of undeserved attack, the blinding instant of unmasked, naked self-awareness.

For those who are willing to let the Word go to their core, there is an extraordinary promise. The first psalm's first words are, "Blessed is the person." What is it to be blessed, to be, as Peterson says, "lucky with holy luck"?[16] It is partly, but not wholly, to be fruitful and prosperous (v. 3). The essence of God's blessing awaits verse 6: "For the LORD knows the way of the righteous."

There's nothing more basic than this question: Does God know me? The Hebrew *yadah* here carries all the affective, relational freight it has, for example, in the Garden, where Adam "knows" Eve, and she bears a child.

How different this blessedness is from a utilitarian vision of self-generated "happiness," how wholly other from gnostic pride's self-evaluation. It's too easy to seek what Pinocchio sought: self-made personhood. All he got for his trouble was a long nose and an increasingly wooden heart. What he needed was to turn to Geppetto, his maker and potential father, and allow himself to be known, that is, to be loved. It's no different with us. The Maker's knowing makes us more than puppets. It's in praise and thanks that we know his Fatherly love.

God's Song and My Song

We are all inveterate idolators, little Pinocchios trying to work our way from puppethood to independent personhood. In this chapter I want to confess my own false gods, because my passion for the importance of a sung theology lies in the way God has used music and song to carry out his campaign against my pet idols. Others may worship elsewhere, but I worship at the twin altars of Reason and Action—also known as Knowing and Doing.

I came to Christianity in the first place in pursuit of Idol #1, a tidy intellectual universe. I had read enough my senior year in high school—chiefly, James Michener's *Fires of Spring*, Nikos Kazantzakis's *Last Temptation of Christ*, and Erich Fromm's *Psychoanalysis and Religion*—to realize my worldview was not quite coherent. I felt it needed at least a little tweaking, maybe more. Enter the Christians, apparently the only kind of people I could meet my freshman year in college. With them came claims on behalf of stubbornly historic, biblical Christianity. No one articulated those claims more winsomely, if doggedly, than a pastor named Mort Whitman, himself a student of the brisk Calvinism of Francis Schaeffer and Cornelius Van Til.

In his book *Orthodoxy*, G. K. Chesterton describes the intellectual quest that brought him to Christianity. He says he was converted to Christianity because it happened to answer exactly to the portrait of God he had already imagined.[17] I find that to be most remarkable. My experience was precisely the opposite—the God I found was the last thing I was looking for. I sought some great Archimedean point in the sky, a divine Answer Man. Instead, I was found by a God with wounds.

One night Mort heard me sing and play on the guitar one of the many love songs I knew. "From the way you seemed to feel that song, it sounds like you're going to need a bigger God than just Someone who can explain why $E=mc^2$ works," he mused. "Okay, but what did you think of the song?" was my rejoinder, but some other voice inside me muttered, "So he knows." Finally, there was the night Mort, frustrated after an extended conversation about whether God existed, blurted, "Reggie, I think you worship your doubts. Could it be you just enjoy being the aloof inquirer?" While part of me looked for a clever repartee, a deeper part confessed, "He's right." My intellectual curiosity was a smoke screen for a psyche that wanted to stay untethered. I wanted a God I could manage, not a God who would meddle. I was having a hard time admitting that I needed a God who would do a lot more than meddle—that I needed the God who had scarred himself to heal the broken and out-of-control places I hid from everybody else. Within a few days, I succumbed to Christ, figuring that any remaining riddles needed to be worked out from the inside of the faith. I sensed it was wiser to accept faith's mystery than continue in unfaith's befuddlement. I was starved for what Mort's intrusive God offered.

In what was to be a long-term stroke of providence, Mort recruited me to play guitar for the worship services of the Orthodox

Presbyterian church he was planting. The church rented space from a synagogue; the only instrumentation we had was what we brought with us on Sundays. Early each week Mort would give me hymn numbers and a list of praise songs for which we had lyric and chord sheets. I would work out the chords of the hymns and write them in the hymnal. Thus began a long tutelage in musical worship that bridges hymnody and contemporary song. I had wanted a simple worldview-adjustment, but God was out to do some de- and reconstructing of my innards. It didn't seem like such a big thing back then, but music of the faith was to take center stage in that worldview formation.

My first inkling came in December of that same freshman year, the night Mort took me to hear the college choir's performance of Handel's *Messiah*. Following my surrender to Christ, I had gone on to complete an otherwise discouraging first semester. (It seems Christian salvation does not include rescue from the consequences of irresponsible study habits.) As this was to be my first Christmas in Christ, Mort wanted me to go into it with Handel's classic ringing in my ears.

I was completely unprepared for the experience. It's not that I had never heard any of the music before. But I had never heard it in context, all at once, or, more importantly, from the inside, from a posture of faith. Minutes into the program I was weeping. I was overwhelmed by the beauty, the majesty, the poetry, the melding of passion and thoughtfulness, of loveliness and truth—the things that make Handel's *Messiah* the special phenomenon it is. I felt bathed in a new existential awareness: what Christ brought was more than truths to learn or disciplines to master. It was more like his coming made me—made all of us—the object of a passionate courtship. That night God shot his arrow into my "guts," to use the New Testament's precise, if inelegant, term (*splanchna*) for "the place where you feel."

In the years since, all kinds of songs have kept God in my *splanchna*. But the Psalms have anchored my soul. It was ad hoc strumming through Psalms that got me through that roadside night in Virginia. In graduate school, it was the folk settings of psalms by the St. Louis Jesuits that kept my faith from being ship-wrecked. My preparation for teaching worship at the seminary level brought me to Calvin's Geneva and that church's reveling in the singing of metrical psalms. It has been a delight to sing with my students Louis Bourgeois's dancelike version of Psalm 47 ("Peoples, Clap Your Hands").[18] Among others, we have especially enjoyed singing Calvin Seerveld's setting of Geneva's Psalm 105, a psalm that recites the history of salvation from creation through the exodus.[19] The song is a romp—no wonder Queen Elizabeth I sneered at "Geneva jigs."

In recent years, my friend Jim Hart has introduced me to Sim-plified Anglican Chant.[20] Chant allows you to give the quality of song to any text—poetry or prose—without worrying about the meter of standard musical notation. In simplified chant, you stay on one note until you come to the last word or phrase of a thought, and then you move to a nearby note to complete that thought. In more complex chant forms there is extra movement toward the end of a thought, but the idea is the same.[21] The text, not the music, controls the meter. There is nothing holy about chant as such; yet its "otherness" has the capacity to remind us of mystery. I can understand why the ancients read their sacred texts this way—something in me is saying "Yes" to the text when I commit vocal cords to this strange musical language.

Many so-called praise and worship songs evoke the Psalms by way of citing lines or by massaging particular thoughts. Mi-chael W. Smith's "How Majestic," for instance, begins with the first line of Psalm 8 ("O Lord, our Lord, how majestic is your name in all the earth") and adds phrases from Isaiah 9's prophecy of the coming of Jesus ("Prince of Peace, Mighty God").[22] It's a combination that points to Hebrews 2 and its amazingly dense and complicated clustering of the themes of the majesty of God and the dignity of the human race, a dignity lost but then restored in Jesus. Maybe a traditional hymn writer could unpack all that without making things too turgid. But Smith's allusiveness has its own power.

Chris Tomlin's "Forever" is a splendid evocation of the spirit of Psalm 136. That psalm recites God's history with his people, from creation through the exodus, the conquest, and his daily provision, and constantly punctuates the history with praise, "The steadfast love of the Lord endures forever." By contrast, Tomlin's song alludes to God's acts in a more general way and gives more room to the acclamation.

> Give thanks to the Lord, our God and King—
> His love endures forever.
> For he is good, he is above all things—
> His love endures forever . . .
>
> With a mighty hand and outstretched arm—
> His love endures forever.
> For the life that's been reborn—
> His love endures forever.

The oft-repeated refrain, "His love endures forever," gives way to a more extended chorus:

> Sing praise. Sing praise.
> Forever God is faithful.
> Forever God is strong.
> Forever God is with us. Forever.[23]

My community of worship laces the song with a vigorous congregational reading of the Nicene Creed. Even without the creed, though, the song suggests the pattern of Psalm 136. It makes that

psalm's story present to us and allows us to linger on the giving
of thanks.

God's War Songs

If Psalm 1 weds mind and heart, Psalm 2 joins action and
affect. Psalm 2 sets the Psalms into the framework of how God
is governing his universe. Psalms are sung by souls caught up
in a cosmic struggle. Like the tales about Tolkien's diminutive
hobbits, my own little story is cast against the backdrop of large
forces, some seen, some unseen, some hostile, some friendly.
Somehow, my little life, its daily store of small acts of obedience
and rebellion, are part of a great campaign God is waging. I sing
because I am part of his army on the march. I sing so I will have
the courage for today's battle, so I will not turn and run when
the enemy is engaged.

Psalm 2 opens with the incredulous question: why does the
human race hate God so (vv. 1–3)? Why are its powers and all its
peoples—otherwise at war with one another—united in this one
thing: to overthrow God and his Anointed One?

This is a bracing feature of biblical song: God's songs are not
celestial Valium. Rather than sugarcoat the human condition, the
Psalms look into the cosmically rebellious human breast with eyes
wide open. They sing a brand of blues so raw and honest they
would make blues singer John Lee Hooker blush. But there is a
reason the Psalms can gaze so honestly and sing so bluely. They
know a secret. "Guess what?" they wink. "God wins. Darkness
loses. Praise be."

Psalm 2 has two sister psalms: Psalm 37 and Psalm 59. Psalm
37 is the source for Jesus's teaching that "the meek shall inherit
the earth"; however, it acknowledges that for now, "The wicked
plot against the just, and gnash their teeth at them."[24] For its part,
Psalm 59 is one of several that David pens after Samuel anoints

him but before he becomes king. During this time the reigning King Saul is trying to kill him. David's song rages against the "wicked transgressors":

> At evening they return,
> They growl like a dog,
> And go all around the city.
> Indeed, they belch with their mouth;
> Swords are in their lips;
> For they say, "Who hears?"
>
> vv. 6–7 NKJV

Each of these three psalms has a simple response to the horror described.

Psalm 2:4 says: "God laughs."
Psalm 37:13 says: "God laughs."
Psalm 59:8 says—that's right—"God laughs."

Derisively, mockingly, God laughs. The early Christians recognized the fulfillment of Psalm 2:1–3 in the plot of Herod and Jesus's countrymen and Pilate and the Gentiles. The plotters of the death of God's Anointed had, quite despite themselves, done God's preordained will. In the end, when humans try to thwart God's purpose, they merely work his mysterious will (see Acts 4:25–28).

Psalms like these three take us above the fray. They provide altitude for our struggles. They invite us to share God's laughter. Though it may sound immodest and sub-Christian, there is a sense in which God invites us to share his mockery of his stupidly shortsighted enemies. When we sing God's song we take up his laughter, and it is partly a laughter of derision, of "taunting"—precisely in the sense in which the term is used in sports these days.

In reality, the joke is on us too. The title of a lesser known 1970s Broadway musical about the life of Jesus says it well: "Your Arms Too Short to Box with God."[25] We have all tried to box with God. When we realize how comical it is to contest his rulership, he says—amazingly, graciously—"Now you laugh too."

But why can God laugh? And why can we laugh with him? Psalm 2 speaks of God installing his Son as King on Mt. Zion:

> "I have installed My King
> Upon Zion, My holy mountain."
> I will surely tell of the decree of the LORD:
> He said to me, "You are My Son,
> Today I have begotten You."
>
> Psalm 2:6–7 NASB

Paul says this happened when God raised Jesus from the dead:

> And we preach to you the good news of the promise made to the fathers, that God has fulfilled this promise to our children in that He raised up Jesus, as it is also written in the second Psalm, "You are My Son; today I have begotten you."
>
> Acts 13:32–33 NASB

In this claim that Jesus's resurrection was the day of God's installing his Son as King lies the key to an apparent enigma at the end of the Psalter. Why does the Psalter end with such exuberant, triumphant praise? As we saw earlier, when we follow the Psalter's outline we find ourselves caught up in a story of God's taking his people from shame to glory, and from complaint to praise. After David's sufferings (Book One), there is the establishment of his reign and its transfer to Solomon (Book Two). Solomon fails to follow God wholeheartedly; and the breakup of David's dynasty leads eventually to exile (Book Three). During the exile,

Israel is reminded that God is the nation's true King (Book Four). Even so, after exile is ended, hope is reborn that God's rule will be expressed through "a horn for his people," and that all the earth—indeed creation itself—will rejoice because a King reigns in Zion (Book Five).

The first two and the last five psalms bracket this mini-narrative perfectly. Just as the first two psalms seem to serve as an introduction to the whole of the Psalter, the last five, all of them so-called "Hallelujah" psalms, appear to have been placed, perhaps even composed, as a fitting closing for the Psalter.[26] They make a handsome bookend with the opening psalms. We begin the Psalter reading Scripture reflectively, sitting to plant ourselves deeply in God's Word. We finish the Psalter singing, dancing, and playing musical instruments, as we rise to call the very heavens to jubilant praise. Psalm 2 begins with the faithful cowering before the dark powers that stand against God and his Anointed. Psalm 149 ends with God's opponents being wiped out while the "godly ones" are crowned with honor.

But the praise at the close of the Psalter doesn't match the facts of Israel's history. During the era in which the Psalter is finalized, Israel has indeed returned from exile, and the temple is being reconstructed. But, as the prophets admit, the glory of the second temple is nothing like that of the first. Nor is there a return of the Davidic line—Israel is a vassal of the Persian Empire, and the Persians are not about to permit a renewed Davidic kingship.

So why the effusive outpouring of praise at the end? Psalms 146–150, it seems to me, are psalms that look to the end of history. The final cluster of psalms opens out onto a promise that transcends the boundaries of Israel's history. Israel's journey was a pilgrimage that awaited another chapter: the day when God would, as Psalm 2 promised, raise up Messiah. God's people drafted the Psalter to sustain themselves in that hope. They knew that one day God and they would have the last laugh. Centuries later, the early believers of Acts 4 recognized that when God raised his Son from the dead, the time for laughter had come.

Christianity: Only a Credo? Only a Manifesto?

After I had been a Christian for a year or two, I picked up Idol #2: I became committed to—no, obsessed with—the quest for social justice. I was after what Christian social activist Jim Wallis once called "God's agenda for biblical people." My college years bridged the late 1960s and early 1970s, and though a lot of folks around me were angry about Vietnam, I was more shamed by my country's and especially my region's racism (my family is from the Deep South). My zeal over race left me with little energy for other spiritual priorities, whether personal holiness or individual evangelism.

A simple remark by a college classmate marked a turning point. In our senior year, a friend named Lauren and I were the lone evangelicals in a seminar course on modern theology. This particular week, we were reading a Marxist theologian of liberation. My chief aims in this discussion were: first, to prove to my way-left-of-center professor that being an evangelical was not an act of intellectual suicide, and, second, to demonstrate to my antiestablishment fellow students that Bible-believing Christians were also concerned about the evils of social injustice. Sometimes Lauren's faith seemed embarrassingly simple to me, and especially on the day we discussed this Marxist theologian.

Nearly all I remember from the class's reaction to the book was the shared anger, our despair over the stubbornness of inequity, and our resentment that the "haves" of the world could not see life from the other side. Finally, Lauren spoke up: "The thing that troubles me about this book and the approach to God it represents is that, well, there's no joy in it. There doesn't seem to be anything to celebrate."

At first I thought, *What an odd thing to say. Just one more confirmation that Christians are so heavenly minded they are no earthly good.* But then I realized the point of her protest. The theologian we were discussing had so abridged the faith that all that was left was a political platform. There was nothing in his mandate for change that merited the *theo*-part of his "theology" of liberation. There was no sense that what gave hope for change in this world was Christ's victory over the grave and all the forces of hell.

It is hard to explain why, but the flashpoint was remembering the many, many settings in which Lauren and I had sat with other believers around that campus and sung the faith. In an instant in that classroom I had a picture of the way our lives were being transformed to serve humankind through submission to the interests of the City of God—specifically, through joyful worship of the Messiah whom God had raised from the dead and made Lord of the nations.

Though I was not able to articulate it at the time, afterward as I pondered the way song came to mind at that moment, I thought, *Isn't there, after all, something about Christianity that has at its heart celebration, precisely where we have to face how terrible, how unjust, and how unfair life is? Did God intend to give us only something to die for, or if, heaven forbid, our Marxist author was right, something to kill for but nothing to live for? Only anger, no joy? Only a manifesto, no song?*

I realized then that our outlook on history and society is anchored in the conviction that above us stands a God who laughs. He mocks the arrogance of the exploiters who misperceive the kind restraint of his wrath and refuse to repent (Rom. 2:4–5). He laughs at the folly of sin's residuum in a redeemed person's racism. He scoffs at the demons who mock my redemption, as though the besetting sins I have yet to shake in thirty years of following Christ could lessen my Father's commitment to see my salvation through. God chortles at the way those same voices try to keep me looking back over my shoulder at the many places I could have—should have—zigged but zagged instead. As if anything could keep him from directing my steps despite whatever inanity goes into how I plan the way (Prov. 16:9).

Lauren's question has energized me for years. To be sure, the manifesto is there: the call to the City of God carries its pilgrims through both the business district and the slums of the City of Man. Christ cares about what is happening in the City of Man. We are called to stand up to tyrants and to help people through the tumults, the strife, and the darkness. Pilgrims on the way, we are called to give up everything—including life itself—for the sake of the gospel's call. But our pilgrimage is a pilgrimage of joy, and it needs to be carried by song.

Too many of us, it seems to me, are trying to make it through all this with tight jaws, pursed lips, and angry spirits. We are ready to die the martyr's death, but we have not learned to sing the martyr's song. For myself, I've had to think of it in these terms: God does not intend me to be a philosopher with no soul, an evangelist with no good news for my own heart, an activist scared to death to look inside.

There is more than enough empty bluster going around these modern and postmodern times. Nonetheless, there is a divine corollary to the braggadocio that surrounds us, for God is at war for and with the nations. Part of his battle is for the little bit of turf that is my breast. I need to hear God's songs recount the footsteps of his march through history, so I can be filled with his bravado, taking what the hymn writer calls "strength for today, and bright hope for tomorrow." God's songs offer me a perspective alongside the One who governs all and who is working his good pleasure right where Satan seems most in control.

Good News for the Weary Warrior

What Psalm 2 intimates is the incredible power all the psalms have for filling us with God's bravado. Mendelssohn understood. I think it's because he himself was prone to depression that the composer identified with the prophet Elijah's need for a pity party and a nap after the conflict with the prophets of Baal and before the confrontation with the more intimidating Jezebel. That's why in his *Elijah* oratorio Mendelssohn was able to select the perfect words for the moment when, according to 1 Kings 19:5, an angel wakes Elijah up, brings him food, and helps him get on his way. As though he knew the need for this comfort himself, Mendelssohn has his angelic corps sing an adaptation of the first four verses of Psalm 121:

> Lift thine eyes to the mountains; whence cometh help?
> Thy help cometh from the Lord, the Maker of heaven and
>   earth.
> He hath said, thy foot shall not be moved, thy Keeper will never
>   slumber.
> He, watching over Israel, slumbers not, nor sleeps.
> Shouldst thou, walking in grief, languish, He will quicken thee.

Whenever it's time for a big task or a stressful obligation, my own escape route of choice is the same as Elijah's: "I need a nap." Sometimes though, I remember Mendelssohn's implicit good news for the weary warrior: "Your Warrior God doesn't need a nap." Then I can stay awake and at my post.

Martin Luther's grief and anger over the martyrdom of two fellow Augustinian monks who refused to recant their "Lutheran" heresy drove him to pen a twelve-verse folk song, folk songs being the most common form of mass communication in his day. This broadsheet recounting and celebrating their martyrdom became the first hymn of the Reformation:

A new song here shall be begun—
The Lord God help our singing!
Of what our God himself hath done,
Praise, honor to him bringing.
At Brussels in the Netherlands,
By two boys, martyrs youthful,
He showed the wonders of his hands,
Whom he with favor truthful
So richly hath adorned.[27]

The year was 1523. Four or five years later, Luther decided to interpret and apply Psalm 46 to the struggles of the church in his day. The result is the text we know as "A Mighty Fortress Is Our God." For its musical setting he adapted the tune from the martyrdom broadsheet. I don't know what brought it to mind; perhaps a line from the older song, "The ancient foe it filled with hate." And nobody seems to know for sure whether that first tune was one he had written himself or had borrowed from someplace else. Regardless, "A Mighty Fortress" is a remarkable combination of tune and psalm text that has served ever since as a rallying cry for defenders of the liberty of the gospel.

A companion piece is Kemper Crabb's anthem "Warrior," a pastiche of images drawn from various places, but chiefly Exodus 15:3 and Psalm 24:8.[28]

The Lord is a Warrior.
The Lord is mighty in battle.
The Lord is a Warrior,
Lord of Hosts is He.

My Lord is a fortress.
He is a Sun and a Shield.
The Lord is a Deliverer
To those who put their trust in Him.

> He gives strength unto His people.
> He guards His own with His Right Hand.
> The angel of the Lord camps
> Around the ones who fear Him,
> And delivers them.

This is bracing stuff, and so is its musical interpretation both by Crabb and by Caedmon's Call.[29] Juxtaposed in worship, Luther's hymn and Crabb's praise song combine to help us participate in God's holy laughter.

As they take up God's war cry and orient me toward his prophetic doings in the world, the songs of Zion give meaning to my own doings in God's world. The songs of the people of God are like the soundtrack to an incredible epic, infinitely grander, earthier, bloodier, and more redemptive than *Braveheart*. Mel Gibson's version of William Wallace's cry of "Freedom!" from the gibbet is but a pale reflection of Christ's cry from the tree: "It is finished!" And if you cannot imagine *Braveheart* without the haunting sounds of the orchestra and uilleann pipes, try imagining the drama of Paradise Lost and Regained—imagine the story line of the Bible and world history—without the soundtrack of the songs of Israel and the church.

Psalm 1 tells us that God simply does not care to satisfy the intellectual curiosity of coolly aloof inquirers: his passion is for dragging ugly wallflowers onto the dance floor. When we come to him looking merely for a respectable philosophical system, he not so subtly reshapes the question: "So it's truth you think you want? Come sing in my choir, then we'll talk." In other words, learn to praise. Understanding will follow.

Psalm 2 informs us that the God of the Bible does not accommodate himself to the agenda of people looking merely for a set of moral principles or guidelines for action. God is working his own deal in history. Graciously and purposefully, he grafts our stories into his. But it is his script—not ours. He teaches us his song so we will know our parts. God makes us over from the inside out, making himself our agenda.

The book of Psalms, though it was finished five centuries after his career, was David's project from beginning to end. It was during his time that Israel learned to sing. Nobody has more to teach us about how to sing our faith than Israel's singing warrior-king. In the next chapter, we will see how David brought new candor to a relationship with God.

3

DAVID

Israel's Sweet Singer and Architect of Praise

A s chief author and sponsor of the Psalter, David is the biblical model of how a person relates to God through song. Of all the people in the Bible, he is easily the most lifelike—and the most likely to break into song.

The wildest extremes of the human experience come together in David. He is failure and triumph, loner and communitarian, fugitive and king. For three millennia, Jewish and Christian parents have taught their children to emulate his greatness and avoid his failings. Of him, biblical scholar Baruch Halpern rightly says:

> David, in a word, is human, fully, four-dimensionally, recognizably human. He grows, he learns, he travails, he triumphs, and he suffers immeasurable tragedy and loss. He is the first human being in world literature.[1]

David is warrior and poet, friend and rogue. He boasts both of fingers skilled at the ten-stringed harp and of arms trained to bend the bronze bow (Pss. 144:9; 18:34). The Bible calls him a man after God's heart (Acts 13:22) but also says that his hands were so defiled from bloodshed he was disqualified from fulfilling one of his heart's deepest desires, building a temple to God (1 Chron. 28:3; 2 Chron. 6:7–8). David is jubilant to the point of immodesty at the return of the ark of the covenant from the Philistines but melancholic to the point of suicidal depression at the death of Absalom, his traitor-son. He is basely cruel in his adultery with Bathsheba and in the murder of her husband, Uriah, yet movingly compassionate in caring for Mephibosheth, lame son of his friend Jonathan.

When we look closely at David's life and his psalms, two instructive portraits emerge. One is a plaintive and personal portrayal of a suffering saint. This is the David of 1 and 2 Samuel and of the thirteen psalms that claim a specific location in these books. It is significant that in this narrative strand David is called the "Sweet Singer of Israel" (2 Sam. 23:1). Through song, he relentlessly pursues the Lord in the midst of travails, while his inner person is being molded and shaped by his God.

The second portrait, for which I use the term "Architect of Praise," is that of a righteous king who bequeaths a musical tradition to his beloved Israel. This portrait comes to us in the remembrances of David compiled after the Babylonian captivity: 1 and 2 Chronicles. Here the history writers focus on David as the one who has overcome his enemies, established his kingdom, and inaugurated a grand season of praise. While the writers of this era cite Moses as their authority on other aspects of worship, they cite David as their authority on how they should sing. Here it becomes clear that his songs are the most abiding contribution he makes to the construction of God's house. Here is where David's songs become our songs.

In a sense, the pilgrimage from suffering to glory we see in the book of Psalms is personified in David. All of Israel's glory and all her failings reside in him. Further, while David's story is uniquely his own, it is also ours. Through the narratives of his life and through the songs he leaves behind, all of God's people learn to sing their pilgrimage.

Israel's Sweet Singer

While 1 and 2 Samuel did not appear as complete books until much later, scholars believe the events of David's life that they recount were probably first written down while Solomon was securing his reign.[2] The stories are intimate and revealing because memories are fresh. Still, it wasn't until five hundred years later, during the Babylonian captivity, that the larger narrative of which 1 and 2 Samuel's account of David's life is but a part—the whole of 1 and 2 Samuel, plus 1 and 2 Kings—was compiled and published. Second Kings ends, in fact, with Judah still in captivity (see 2 Kings 25). The Samuel/Kings narrative is thus history as remembered by a people who value the presence of God above all else but who feel keenly the loss of fellowship with God in the temple in Jerusalem. This setting profoundly affects the way David's story is told. The struggling side of David—the refugee, the repenter, the confused father—brings consolation during exile. The mood surrounding the Samuel/Kings history is perfectly captured in Psalm 137, also written after Jerusalem's fall in 587 BC:

By the rivers of Babylon,
There we sat down, yea, we wept
When we remembered Zion.
We hung our harps
Upon the willows in the midst of it.

For there those who carried us away captive asked of us a song,
And those who plundered us requested mirth,
Saying, "Sing us one of the songs of Zion!"
How shall we sing the LORD's song
In a foreign land?

                                                    vv. 1–4 NKJV

During the captivity, the celebratory aspects of David's reign
are a memory, not a present reality. The Samuel/Kings account is
subdued when it comes to music and song. Israel's Sweet Singer is
primarily remembered as Saul's soul-soother and as the one who
is constantly delivered from enemies. Thus this first portrait is
intimate, melancholic, fascinated with David's fears and foibles
and struggles.

In his youth, David is recruited to play and sing in Saul's household. Saul's handlers hope that the boy's songs can keep at bay
the beasts within that troubled king's soul (1 Sam. 16:14–23). We
haven't been left with any songs from David's days of singing to
Saul, but in an unforgettable painting by Rembrandt, we get a
sense of what the atmosphere must have been. While the old king
uses a curtain to wipe his tears with one hand, he allows his other
hand to relax its grip on his sceptre. Meanwhile, with downcast
adolescent face, David appears to be lost in thought, his own
fingers gracefully strumming his lyre. What's he thinking about?
The terrors in the recesses of Saul's heart? The power of music and
song to touch those secret places? David's own stirrings of desire
for power, for love, for the ability to express it all to the One who
alone knows, understands, cares, and consoles?

Beyond this, the narrative of 1 and 2 Samuel tells us little about
David's music. For this, we can look to his psalms. Happily, we find
that the headings of some of David's psalms tie them to events as
narrated in 1 and 2 Samuel.[3] Most of the seventy-three psalms that
name David either as author or subject do not specify their time

or place of writing. Fortunately, however, thirteen psalms claim particular locations in the narrative of 1 and 2 Samuel. Each one is a song David wrote about his troubles.[4] When we look at these songs in the flow of his life, we see that though his music was not of much help to Saul, it was David's lifeblood.

When Saul turns against him, even being married to the king's daughter doesn't protect David. He has to be secreted out a window when Saul's men first come after him (1 Sam. 19:11–17). His response is one of the "God laughs" psalms we looked at in the previous chapter, Psalm 59. We can only imagine what it meant to him to sing, "My God in His lovingkindness will meet me," as he fled into an unknown future (Ps. 59:10 NASB).

His flight takes him all the way to the gates of Philistine Gath, where he pretends to be insane, even to the extent of dripping spittle down his beard to prove he is harmless (1 Sam. 21:10–15). He composes Psalm 56 to ask God's mercy. Covering his shame, he knows, is the God who has "taken account of my wanderings; [and] put my tears in [his] bottle" (Ps. 56:8 NASB). He loves the coherence of God's Word all the more—"In God, whose word I praise,/ In the LORD, whose word I praise . . . I have put my trust"—because he has feigned madness before man who has trampled him (compare Ps. 56:1, 4, 10–11). Within the exercise of crafting words to articulate his situation and express his feelings, David arrives at a deeper sense of the veracity of God himself. He can pretend to be confused—even mad—because he knows God's Word is true; and what is happening outside himself does not threaten what is true within himself.

Psalm 34 also comes from this period in David's life when he is seeking asylum as a lunatic. His fool's charade puts him in a unique position to understand that it is the "poor" whom the Lord hears, the "brokenhearted" to whom the Lord is near, and the "crushed in spirit" whom the Lord saves (Ps. 34:17–18).

He hides in caves and is betrayed by bedouins (the Ziphites, see 1 Samuel 23; 26). In Psalm 54, he sings his frustration to God, whom he calls "helper" and the "sustainer of my soul" (v. 4 NASB).

One of the most extraordinary psalms from the days in which he is running from Saul, in my opinion, is Psalm 57. If I were David, I would be trying to keep a low profile, and I'm not sure I would have much energy for personal morning devotions. But even with Saul in hot pursuit, David's mornings are given to praise—loud, exuberant praise:

> Awake, my glory!
> Awake, harp and lyre!
> I will awaken the dawn.
>
> Psalm 57:8 NASB

While I would be looking for a rock to hide under, David seeks refuge in a better place:

> Have mercy on me, O God, have mercy on me,
>   for in you my soul takes refuge.
> I will take refuge in the shadow of your wings
>   until the disaster has passed.
>
> Psalm 57:1 NIV

In a logic comprehensible only to a person who has learned that praise precedes understanding, David says he knows that Saul will fall into a trap of his own making:

> They have prepared a net for my steps;
> My soul is bowed down;
> They dug a pit before me;
> They themselves have fallen into the midst of it.
>
> Psalm 57:6 NASB

Scurrying around in a forced exile that has him bouncing from Moab to Philistia, David sings to the Lord who is over all the nations. Moreover, David makes out ever so faintly a few bars of a symphony of God's mercy that will only find full voice when Jesus, David's greater Son, comes to sing among the nations (Rom. 15:9):

> I will praise You, O Lord, among the peoples;
> I will sing to You among the nations.
> For Your mercy reaches unto the heavens,
> And Your truth unto the clouds.
> Be exalted, O God, above the heavens;
> Let Your glory be above all the earth.
>
> Psalm 57:9–11 NKJV

Twice, the narrator of 1 Samuel tells us, providence delivers Saul into David's hands: once when Saul is relieving himself in a cave where David happens to be hiding, and once when David sneaks into Saul's camp in the middle of the night. Both times David says "No!" to the voice that urges, "Now's your chance. Take him out!" (1 Samuel 24 and 26).

David's refusal to become his own avenger is surprising only if we are not paying attention to his songs. Psalm 142 gives expression to his frustrations and his hopes during these cave-dwelling days. He realizes that "no one cares" for him (Ps. 142:4) and that he is too weak even to face his enemies. But there is hope for release from his wilderness "prison"—not in David's own maneuverings but in the One he calls "my refuge" (v. 5). Ultimately, David believes that he who is "my portion in the land of the living" (v. 5) will take care of his persecutors: "Then the righteous will gather about me because of your goodness to me" (Ps. 142:7 NIV).

Finally Saul falls. David composes Psalm 18, according to the heading, "when the Lord delivered him from the hand of all his enemies and from the hand of Saul" (NIV). This song is one of David's longest and strongest. Here David expresses more vividly than anywhere else the nature of his love for his God:

I love you, O LORD, my strength.
The Lord is my rock, . . . in whom I take refuge.
    He is my shield and the horn of my salvation,
    my stronghold.
I call to the LORD, who is worthy of praise,
    and I am saved from my enemies.

Psalm 18:1–3 NIV

In the twists and turns of his fortunes—embraced and then eschewed by Saul, shunted from Moab to Philistia—David's singing has kept him anchored to a Rock who shows himself "faithful to the faithful, blameless to the blameless, pure to the pure, and shrewd to the crooked" (vv. 25–26). He has been sustained by a vision of a God who saves the humble but brings low the haughty (v. 27). Counter to the gloom that progressively consumed Saul and to the impotence that had Saul falling on his own sword (see 1 Sam. 31:1–7), David knows a God of light and power:

You, O LORD, keep my lamp burning;
    my God turns my darkness into light.
With your help I can advance against a troop;
    with my God I can scale a wall.

Psalm 18:28–29 NIV

Earlier, David had sung God's praises as an exile among the nations. Now, at last, he sings as Israel's head:

Therefore I will praise you among the nations, O LORD;
    I will sing praises to your name.
He gives his king great victories;
    he shows unfailing kindness to his anointed,
    to David and his descendants forever.

Psalm 18:49–50 NIV

However, within chapters of David's coronation, 2 Samuel brings us to David's affair with Bathsheba. Here is David at his most off-putting, imperiously abusive of his power. However, by God's sheer grace one good thing comes from this episode: Psalm 51, David's most soul-searching psalm of repentance. Again, Rembrandt helps us to imagine the poignancy of the scene. Rembrandt captures Bathsheba at her bath reading David's note of invitation. Rembrandt's perspective is painfully voyeuristic, confronting us with the full loveliness David could not resist. We can read the ambivalence in Bathsheba's face as she considers her response. Every time I look at this painting, I recall an interview in which filmmaker Ken Burns describes the filming of the assassination of Abraham Lincoln in his documentary, *The Civil War*. Burns said that in the midst of the filming he was gripped by a fleeting sense that he could intervene and stop the bullet—and how different things would have been. Indeed, what sadness would have been avoided if Bathsheba had written back, "Sorry, no." Or better, if David had simply turned away from the bath scene.

But like the sinners they were—and we all must confess our likeness to them—David and Bathsheba took the shameful path, unleashing a chain of events a Greek tragedian could appreciate. We do not have the words Bathsheba put to her thoughts and feelings. But in Psalm 51 we do have David's, even if his self-examination is prompted only by Nathan's pointed parable about sheep-stealing:

> Deliver me from the guilt of bloodshed, O God,
> The God of my salvation,
> And my tongue shall sing aloud of Your righteousness.
> O Lord, open my lips,
> And my mouth shall show forth Your praise.
> For You do not desire sacrifice, or else I would give it;
> You do not delight in burnt offering.
> The sacrifices of God are a broken spirit,

> A broken and a contrite heart—
> These, O God, You will not despise.
>
> Psalm 51:14–17 NKJV

We learn something amazing here. With a musical instrument in his hands and a song on his lips, this man admits the worst about who he is and what he has done, and in so doing finds greater tenderness and confidence in his relationship with God. David opens the floodgates of the human heart.

Though Psalm 51 is the most notable, psalms of confession stream from this poet's lips and hands all his life:

- Psalm 6—"O LORD, do not rebuke me in your anger" (v. 1 NIV)
- Psalm 32—"Blessed is the one whose transgression is forgiven" (v. 1 NIV)
- Psalm 38—"My guilt has overwhelmed me" (v. 4 NIV)
- Psalm 39—"Save me from all my transgressions" (v. 8 NIV)
- Psalm 40—"My sins have overtaken me, and I cannot see" (v. 12 NIV)
- Psalm 41—"O LORD, have mercy on me; heal me, for I have sinned against you" (v. 4)
- Psalm 51—"Have mercy on me, O God, according to your unfailing love" (v. 1 NIV)
- Psalm 69—"You know my folly, O God; my guilt is not hidden from you" (v. 5 NIV)

This is blues of the deepest sort, blues sad enough to find redemption. If David were indeed a blues singer, he'd be singing about how it's not "the woman's" fault, it's not "demon liquor's" fault, it's not "the Man's" fault—"I been bad all on my own." In a way that is without precedent in the ancient world, David shows how we can come before our Maker and admit that at our core we are not right. All we have to offer is a song from a broken spirit and a contrite heart, and we can know that if we come in this fashion we will not be torn to shreds. David the singer introduces us to the notion that there is a blessedness that awaits those—and only those—who admit that rightness is nowhere within them, who look to God alone to account it to them for no motive besides God's own loving kindness (see Ps. 32:1–5, 10–11).

Sadly, sometimes we find that though a relationship with the Lord grows deeper through confession of sin, the consequences don't always get fixed. It's one of sin's most painful lessons. The lust that sent David after Bathsheba shows up in Amnon, his firstborn son, who longs for and eventually rapes his half sister, Tamar. Tamar's full brother, Absalom, steps in as her champion. He, no doubt, learned much from his father; unfortunately, not all of it good. Singer/songwriter Pierce Pettis perceptively characterizes Absalom:

> You were watching when I took a good man's wife,
> Gave the order for his murder just to cover up the crime.
> All the vanity, cruel arrogance, and greed,
> Oh, Absalom, you learned it all from me.[5]

Absalom avenges Tamar's rape by murdering Amnon. His own sins now having come full circle, David does nothing. Eventually, Absalom starts acting like the king his father will not be and begins to amass a following so he can displace David. David heads back to the caves, this time fleeing his own son. Things are not like they were when he was young; back then, he could just sneak away. Now that he is king, it is a most public event: he has to leave behind ten concubines to satisfy drives in Absalom that David himself has unleashed in this prodigal son. On his way, he allows a Benjamite (and therefore a Saul loyalist) to pelt him with rocks

and curse him as deserving of this degradation.⁶ As humiliating
as the unmasking of his sin with Bathsheba must have been, this
is the nadir of David's reign.

Of all the imaginable responses, the one David makes is the
most surprising: he writes a song. As the heading of Psalm 3 says:
"A Psalm of David, when he fled from Absalom his son" (NASB).
Like nothing else, Psalm 3 reveals what makes David "a man after
God's own heart":

> O LORD, how my adversaries have increased!
> Many are rising up against me.
> Many are saying of my soul,
> "There is no deliverance for him in God."
> But You, O LORD, are a shield about me.
> My glory, and the One who lifts my head.
>
> Psalm 3:1–3 NASB

Fully alive to the hurt, he is even more alive to the reality of the
God who protects and carries him through the disgrace. Psalm 7,
also written during this time, shows a David who is broken to the
core. As a result he can take rebuke when he deserves it; that's why
he accepts the Benjamite's curses and rocks (see 2 Sam. 16:5–13).
Buttressed by God's opinion alone, he can ask the Lord to deflect
blows he does not deserve and to bring an end to the violence
Absalom's rebellion has brought to the land (Ps. 7:9).

In Psalm 63, David sings plaintively about how much he misses
the tabernacle, the place of God's presence: "I have seen you in the
sanctuary and beheld your power and your glory" (Ps. 63:2 NIV).
Just because of that memory, the thirst is all the stronger and the
song all the more soulful: "O God, you are my God, earnestly I
seek you; my soul thirsts for you, my body longs for you, in a dry
and weary land where there is no water" (Ps. 63:1 NIV).

Through it all, David composes and sings with the most remarkable candor and with the most stubborn faith. David's candor, born

in what Michener calls his longing for "the more complete song,"[7] makes him eminently approachable to people who live three thousand years later. I can understand why Bono would call him "the Elvis of the bible [sic]."[8] It's not just that, as Bono points out, the face of Michelangelo's famous sculpture of David bears an uncanny likeness to the first rock-and-roll superstar: David had that same combination of being larger-than-life and as frail as the frailest of us. Perhaps this is why David is the Bible's first real singer.

Israel's Architect of Praise

David's greatest merit—what sets him apart from mere superstardom—is that, as Bono states, "he had the humility of one who knew his gift worked harder than he ever would."[9] When we turn to the recollections of David's career in the chronicles, we see that gift at work. This narrative provides us an entirely different perspective than the one we have seen in the Samuel account, and it is one that, precisely in its differences, shows how one man's song can become everybody's.

The perspective changes in 1 and 2 Chronicles because God's people have undergone a change of address: this portion of Scripture is written after the Babylonian captivity, when the people have returned to the Promised Land. Its mood is captured in the six verses of Psalm 126, which also was written after the exile:

> When the LORD brought back the captives to Zion,
>   we were like men who dreamed.
> Our mouths were filled with laughter,
>   our tongues with songs of joy.
> Then it was said among the nations,
>   "The LORD has done great things for them."
> The LORD has done great things for us,
>   and we are filled with joy.

> Restore our fortunes, O Lord,
>   like streams in the Negev.
> Those who sow in tears
>   will reap with songs of joy.
> He who goes out weeping,
>   carrying seed to sow,
> will return with songs of joy,
>   carrying sheaves with him.
>
>   NIV

Captivity is ended. It is time for "songs of joy." In this era, the final form of the Psalter is taking shape. The temple is being rebuilt. Naturally enough, a different aspect of David emerges. The chroniclers' history is not concerned with David's personal story. This portrait of David is more assured and more communitarian. Though David is indeed banished by Saul, he is hardly running from him—it is more the case that a resistance army is forming around David (see 1 Chronicles 12). Here he is not musician for Saul, refugee in the wilderness, chief repenter in the land, or wounded father. Bathsheba is not even mentioned. Absalom is simply listed as one of David's sons (1 Chron. 3:2).[10] When it comes to music, we see a David who bequeaths the gift of song to his community. Instead of having to piece together David's singing career by correlating psalms with narrative events, we are provided an extended remembrance of David as inaugurator of Israel's great era of song. Here David is "Architect of Praise."

The post-captivity perspective of the Chronicles history becomes apparent in the recounting of any number of events. The account of David's bringing the ark back to Jerusalem from Philistia is especially revealing. Second Samuel focuses on the question of whether it is beneath David's dignity to dance before the ark. David's willingness to appear undignified in his worship of the Lord fits the narrative concerns of the Samuel/Kings history perfectly (2 Sam. 6:12–23). Instead, 1 Chronicles focuses on the music.

Both accounts record the fact that musical praise accompanies the ark's return. By comparison, though, the musical theme in 2 Samuel is understated. According to 2 Samuel 6:15, the procession goes up to Jerusalem simply with "shouts and the sound of trumpets" (NIV). This is in stark contrast to the splendid array of "all kinds of instruments of [cypress], and . . . lyres, harps, tambourines, castanets and cymbals" (v. 5 NASB) that had been assembled three months earlier (when Uzzah's presumption caused the procession to be canceled; see 2 Sam. 6:5–11).

In 1 Chronicles the music is the centerpiece of the entire event. Musicians and instruments are everywhere. No fewer than twenty-five singers and instrumentalists are mentioned by name. David tells them he wants them to "raise sounds of joy" (1 Chron. 15:16 NASB).

> Thus all Israel brought up the ark of the covenant of the LORD with shouting, and with sound of the horn, with trumpets, with loud-sounding cymbals, with harps and lyres.
>
> 1 Chronicles 15:28 NASB

When the ark is finally taken into the tabernacle, there is an elaborate worship service. The priests present offerings. David blesses the people and distributes food to them. He appoints leaders of praise. At the climax of the service, he confers on Asaph and his family the responsibility for leading the people's praise (1 Chron. 16:7): "Then on that day David first assigned Asaph and his relatives to give thanks to the LORD" (NASB).

In 1 Chronicles 16:8–36, there follows a song of commissioning. It is a splendid montage of elements that will later appear in Psalms 96, 105, and 106:

Oh give thanks to the LORD, call upon His name;
Make known His deeds among the peoples.
Sing to Him, sing praises to Him;
Speak of all His wonders.

1 Chronicles 16:8–9 NASB; see vv. 8–22,
and compare with Psalm 105:1–2

Sing to the LORD, all the earth;
Proclaim good tidings of His salvation from day to day.

1 Chronicles 16:23 NASB; see vv. 23–33,
and compare with Psalm 96:1–2

O give thanks to the Lord, for he is good;
For his lovingkindness is everlasting.

1 Chronicles 16:34; see vv. 34–36,
and compare with Psalm 106:47–48

So effective is the narrative at indicating the transition in praise-leading authority, that it is not clear from the text whether it is David who sings this song, or Asaph. Scholars disagree.[11] Precisely in the ambiguity lies the beauty of the text: regardless of who sings the song of commissioning, David's ministry of song now belongs, through Asaph, to all the people of God. At the end of the song, the people add their "Amen" and express their own praise. Then David leaves Asaph and his family to their work—the gatekeepers to their gatekeeping, the priests to their offerings, and the musicians to their "trumpets and cymbals for those who should sound aloud, and with instruments for the songs of God" (v. 42 NASB).

Evident in Asaph's commissioning is a striking contrast between the Samuel/Kings perspective and the Chronicles perspective. As the capstone to David's career, 2 Samuel had provided Psalm 18—the psalm celebrating David's deliverance from Saul. Psalm 18 was the chief illustration of what it meant for David to be Israel's Sweet Singer (see 2 Sam. 22). That psalm fit perfectly 2 Samuel's portrayal of David, the sufferer who had prevailed because of God's faithfulness. When the chroniclers show us David and his music, they want us to see how "his gift worked harder than he ever would." The content of the song that marks Asaph's commissioning (1 Chron. 16:8–36) is not about David's deliverance but about Israel's task to take God's song to the nations. And the text seems almost noncommittal as to whether the song comes from David or Asaph.

The point is that David has become the patron of psalmody itself, bequeathing to God's people his personal pattern of praise. From this point David becomes to psalm what Gregory became to chant, St. Denis to gothic architecture, or Henry Ford to industrial manufacture: establisher of a seemingly inexhaustible fund of energy and inspiration.

David's commissioning of Asaph is the beginning of a whole new epoch of corporate worship. Beyond this particular occasion, David aggressively works to leave Israel with a tradition of praise, organizing the Levites with Chenaniah as leader of the singers (1 Chron. 15:27) and setting in place commandments for music-making that would be appealed to in future generations (2 Chron. 23:18; 29:25). The Levites in Solomon's day play "the LORD's musical instruments, which King David had made for praising the LORD and which were used when he gave thanks, saying, 'His love endures forever'" (2 Chron. 7:6 NIV). Three hundred years later, Hezekiah is able to station

the Levites in the temple of the LORD with cymbals, harps and lyres in the way prescribed by David and Gad the king's seer and Nathan the prophet: this was commanded by the LORD through his prophets. So the Levites stood ready with David's instruments, and the priests with their trumpets.

2 Chronicles 29:25–26 NIV

While Moses had told the Levites to present burnt offerings to the Lord, David specifies more precisely the Levites' division of labor, and in addition, insists that the offerings now be made "with rejoicing and singing" (2 Chron. 23:18). He contributes the practice of antiphonal singing (Neh. 12:24). He lays out stations for the instrumentalists to stand in temple worship. He does it so clearly that at the dedication of the foundation of the second temple over five hundred years later, Ezra can have the trumpeters and cymbal players take the very same spots (Ezra 3:10—see also 2 Chron. 35:15).

As no one before him, David realized that the atmosphere of God's presence—and it is God's presence that the ark exists to symbolize—should be made up of song. We know that one of David's greatest desires had been to build a structure more worthy than a mere tent to house the ark of the presence but that God tells him, "No," by virtue of all the blood that it has taken to establish his kingdom. We know that God allows him instead to create the climate and provide the resources so his son Solomon, whose very name means "Peaceful," can build the house.

What the discerning reader comes to see is that God's "No" is a qualified "No." David becomes, so to speak, the temple's acoustical engineer. He designs its "aural architecture": he writes his songs, plays them for the Lord, offers them in service of God's people, and shapes the corporate singing of God's praise. The Psalms themselves are as much a part of the building of God's house as anything else is. David understood that what was to fill God's house was not the smoke from the animal sacrifices, nor the smell of the incense, nor the ark of the covenant, all of which were mere pointers to things beyond themselves. The temple was the meeting place of God and his people because it was to be filled with the realities of the self-offerings and the prayers and the praises of the people on the one hand, and with the Shekinah glory of God's very presence on the other. In Psalm 22:3, David imagines God being enthroned upon praise, not upon individuals' solitary praises but upon the praises of people gathered together in God's house. Because they create "musical space" for the meeting between God and his people, the Psalms—as God's people sing them together—are as vital to the construction of the temple as are the pillars and beams. The Psalms David initiated are the aural architecture of the house of God.

This is a point the chroniclers make clear in their telling of the story of the dedication of the temple. If all we had was the account in 1 Kings, we would never know a single musical note was sounded that day. But in 2 Chronicles we find

> all the Levitical singers, Asaph, Heman, Jeduthun, and their sons and kinsmen, clothed in fine linen, with cymbals, harps and lyres, standing east of the altar, and with them one hundred and twenty priests blowing trumpets in unison when the trumpeters and the singers were to make themselves heard with one voice to praise and to glorify the LORD, and when they lifted up their voice accompanied by trumpets and cymbals and instruments of music, and when they praised the LORD *saying,* "*He* indeed is good for His lovingkindness is everlasting" . . .

Then, and not until then, does the Shekinah-glory cloud show up:

> . . . then the house, the house of the LORD, was filled with a cloud, so that the priests could not stand to minister because of the cloud, for the glory of the LORD filled the house of God.

> 2 Chronicles 5:12–14 NASB

It is as though the passage in 2 Chronicles was intended as a direct fulfillment of the mystery David had articulated at Psalm 22:3, where he had praised God: "You are holy, enthroned on the praises of Israel" (ESV). In the temple dedication service, in about as literal a fashion as can be imagined, God takes his throne on the praises of Israel.

There's more to the story than 1 and 2 Samuel had told us: David was not just a lonely cave dweller, a sinner alone before God ("Against you, you only have I sinned"—Ps. 51:4 NASB), an individual whose heart craved God.[12] The message of the post-captivity historians is this: because David was the Lord's Anointed, he understood that his experience was more than his own. He knew his hunger was not his only, his sins uniquely his alone, or his gift of song for his sole benefit. In their own way, 1 and 2 Chronicles draw our attention to those aspects of David's life that show how much *togetherness* and *connectedness* belong to the biblical picture of salvation. David wanted to be with God among God's people. He wanted God to be renowned in the nations, and he wanted a united Israel to be a showcase of God's mercy, justice, and love. David wanted to be part of a band, not a lonely superstar. He prized the orchestra more than the solo.

Who Is the Real David?

A mystery lurks in the dual portait of David we have seen in this chapter, a tension lying at the heart of Old Testament history. It is as though the question were begging to be asked: Will the real David please stand up? The more individually and plaintively portrayed "Sweet Singer of Israel" of the Samuel/Kings account? The more corporately and triumphantly portrayed institutional-izer of Psalm-singing of the Chronicles narrative?

One way to resolve the tension is to conclude that one or both of the accounts has the whole thing wrong. Perhaps folks who are in exile and who have lost hope write the Samuel/Kings narrative around a whittled down David, a David to match their diminished expectations. Alternatively, maybe a later generation of folks who are returning from exile and are experiencing a wave of patriotism distort things by inflating the glory years of David in the Chronicles narrative. Or perhaps both accounts have it right, and Israel's history is itself thick with the enigma of a complicated redemptive process. I would argue the two narratives complete each other—our angle of vision has to be multi-perspectival. Together the pre-captivity and post-captivity narratives embody a dynamic we have already seen in the structure of the Psalter itself. The Psalter takes shape around Israel's longing to move from shame to glory, from mourning to dancing. David's career is multilayered because he tastes both the suffering and the glory.

While God's people languished in exile they needed to understand what David had learned on the run: the Lord is present to the brokenhearted and the disenfranchised. The exiles' "harps hung on the willows" in the sense that robust, celebrative temple worship was closed off to them. Nonetheless, from David's life they knew theirs was a God of mercy who would draw near to those who adopted a posture of praise and contrition. It's the same for us: precisely when God's hand feels so heavy and his blessing so remote, songs of worship become the means by which we gain perspective and experience restoration of fellowship with the Lord.

The generation of the return from Babylon remembers that joyful song had burst forth under David not just because he was a gifted singer-songwriter. Song had flowered because of a fulness of time in Israel's life under David's reign. Deliverance had reached something of a culmination: God had been near. With David's securing of the borders and his establishment of Jerusalem as the City of God, as "the place" (see Deuteronomy 12) where God would meet with his people, Israel had come to the pinnacle of her history. The chroniclers' narrative of David's life suits a time in which the harps no longer have to hang on branches alongside the Euphrates. The songs of Zion (Ps. 137:3) or the songs of the Lord (2 Chron. 29:27; Ps. 137:4) can be sung again in the house of the Lord because the Lord of the house is back in the house. The people of the return live as had the people of David's day: on the cusp of redemption's realization. Redemption is on the march and God has drawn near. The appropriate response is song. The people of the chroniclers' day remember David's songs, and they sing them again as they rebuild the walls around Jerusalem and reconstruct the temple that the city houses.

The struggling David of Samuel/Kings captures our hearts with his honesty before God, with his dogged determination to be real with the Lord about life's pain, and with his resolve to know at the core of his existence God's goodness. Even given the affinity most of us naturally have with the personal portrait of David in the Samuel/Kings narrative, I would suggest that the chroniclers' account fits our time as well. We are like believers of those days of return from exile. By virtue of Christ's conquest over the grave, we live more in the light of God's presence than in the darkness of his absence or even in the twilight of the aching memory of his presence.

David can embody both these realities because he sang of Another who would drink more deeply than he the cup of suffering and dance more joyously than he the dance of deliverance. In Psalm 22, to which we now turn, he introduces us to his—and our—Singing Savior.

4

PSALM 22

The Musical Hinge

L ife is like a box of chocolates." Sometimes a single line in a
movie is so well crafted and so well delivered that merely
to hear it later is to experience that movie all over again. We may
find ourselves on a bus stop bench listening to Forrest Gump
muse over how wonderfully "fluky" life can be.

Psalm 22 is like one of these great one-liners: simultaneously
one of David's most painful and most hopeful songs, it crystal-
lizes the two portraits of David as Sweet Singer and Architect of
Praise.

Exquisitely, Psalm 22 encapsulates the Psalter's theology of
Israel's journey from shame to glory, revealing fascinating insights
into how we can expect life with God to proceed.

Beyond that, Psalm 22 anticipates the song of our Savior, Jesus
Christ. From its opening cry of despair to its victorious conclu-

sion, this psalm prophesies a thousand years in advance both the means of Jesus's execution ("They pierced my hands and feet") and his role as lead worshiper in the church following his resurrection.

"Why Have You Forsaken Me?"

Psalm 22 opens with the most desperate fear a person who has staked his existence on the being and provision of Deity can have: being left alone—cosmically, really alone:

> My God, my God, why have You forsaken me?
> Far from my deliverance are the words of my groaning.
> O my God, I cry by day, but You do not answer;
> And by night, but I have no rest.

vv. 1–2 NASB

The first two-thirds of the psalm rehearse an unrelieved litany of personal disaster. It is impossible to ascertain the exact scenario, but David is in trouble. From the portrait we've seen in the Samuel/Kings history and in the thirteen psalms tied to that history, this is a familiar situation. Part of this song's power is that David sings about his trouble in metaphorical rather than literal terms. "I am poured out like water," he cries, "dogs surround me." This language makes it easier for us to transfer the psalm into our own experience when we're in a hard place.

Enemies have cut David off from any help. They're as strong as bulls and roar like a lion. They have already pierced his hands and feet. Now they leer at him and taunt him as death closes in; he is not dead yet, but he senses them already dividing up his clothes. We don't know if his enemies are Saul and his henchmen, some Moabite horde, or Absalom and his courtiers. Regardless, he feels as though God has pulled away to let them have their way with him.

This is a strange feeling for David. He is accustomed to God's presence and protection. He has known God's care from infancy, and he knows himself to be immersed in a history of God's nurture of his people (see verses 4–5 and 9–10).

As he feels God slipping away, though, David stubbornly refuses to let go of him. God lives—indeed, he reigns—in the place where his people praise him. David remembers the sanctuary where God meets his people. He remembers the songs that facilitate the meeting. Into what he perceives to be the silence of God, he sings:

> Yet You are holy,
> O You who are enthroned upon the praises of Israel.
> In You our fathers trusted;
> They trusted and You delivered them.
>
> vv. 3–4 NASB

This instinct for song at such a moment is why the Samuel/Kings narrative dubs David "Israel's Sweet Singer." In the song David's attention swings back and forth between his plight (vv. 1–2, 6–8, 12–18) and the God who could rescue him if only he would (vv. 3–5, 9–11, 19–21).[1] The sections that focus on David himself get longer and more graphic. Nonetheless, David keeps coming back to the God who has apparently abandoned him and who seems to be laying him in "the dust of death" (v. 15).

The sections of the petition that focus on God move from the most exalted attribute—God's holiness (v. 3)—to his more approachable attributes—the faithfulness with which he has cared for his people in history (vv. 4–5) and the tenderness with which he has provided for David, at least up to now (vv. 9–10). Finally, David offers a desperate plea for God to intervene (vv. 19–21).

In Hebrew poetry ideas rhyme, not words. David's poetic touch is staggeringly beautiful. Beginning in verse 12, he gradually introduces his tormenters: bulls of Bashan, a roaring lion, a pack of dogs, those who pierce his hands and feet. In verses 20–21 (NKJV) in reverse order and staccato fashion, he begs God,

> Deliver Me from the sword,
> My precious life from the power of the dog.
> Save Me from the lion's mouth
> And from the horns of the wild oxen!

The last word in verse 21 is the turning point of the psalm. With David's enemies closing in for the kill, God provides a last-minute deliverance, and David responds with a single-word cry, 'ănîtánî: "You-have-answered-me!"[2] Using the same verb, David had complained in verse 2, "O my God, I cry by day, but you do not answer" (lō' ta'ăneʰ). Now he realizes God has been listening after all.

"I Will Sing Hymns"

The dramatic "You-have-answered-me" is followed by a sudden shift of scene. David is so excited about God's deliverance that he calls for a national feast day—actually, a worldwide feast day. David stands at the head of the feast table and calls on people to join him in worship. A song that had begun as a lament of abandonment turns into a victory chant, a promise to the Lord that all the families of the earth will join in praise: "For the kingdom is the LORD's, and He rules over the nations" (v. 28 NKJV).

In fulfillment of a vow apparently made during the peril, David offers a sacrifice of thanksgiving for his deliverance: "From You comes my praise in the great assembly; I shall pay my vows before those who fear Him" (v. 25 NASB).[3] Mosaic law provides such "votive sacrifices" for people to pledge their faithfulness to God, and "thank offerings" for people to express gratitude to God when he makes unusual provisions. According to Moses, thanksgiving feasts like this should last no more than two days (Lev. 7:16); they should take place in Jerusalem if possible (Deuteronomy 12) and should include one's family members. Elsewhere in the book of Psalms we see that votive and thank offerings were public events, occasions for extolling the merits of the God who saves (e.g., Pss. 13:6; 27:6). The royal party occasioned by the deliverance that Psalm 22 celebrates is a public event. In this setting David shouts:

> I will declare Your name to my brothers;
> In the midst of the assembly I will sing hymns to you.
>
> verse 22

The elements of the worship that David commends in the last third of this psalm are various: praise, doxology, standing in awe, the paying of vows, eating and being satisfied, remembering and turning to the Lord, worshiping, bowing, serving, declaring the Lord's righteousness.

Especially noteworthy is the spectrum of people on David's praise-party guest list. In fact, a fine poetic structure frames the concluding verses of this psalm—a series of sociological contrasts between the groups that make up what he calls his "great assembly" (v. 25). David's gathering can be mapped out this way:

- Israelites: "the descendants of Jacob"; "the offspring of Israel" (v. 23 NKJV)
- The poor: "the Afflicted" (vv. 24–26 NKJV)
- Gentiles: "the ends of the earth"; "the families of the nations" (vv. 27–28 NKJV)
- The rich: "the fat ones of the earth" (v. 29)
- The dead: "those who go down to the dust" (v. 29 NKJV)
- The unborn: "a people not yet born" (vv. 30–31)

With an elegant sense of style, David describes a community of worship in which Israelites are complemented by Gentiles, the poor by the rich, and the dead by the not yet born. Distinctive to this psalm is the way David sees in his own rescue a glimpse into the way God delivers others, beginning with Israel's faithful and poor but finally including everyone.

Offspring of Israel and Families of the Nations

David calls for worship from the people who know God by covenant. In this way the "descendants of Jacob" and the "offspring of Israel" share David's story. In his own deliverance David hears an echo of Israel's rescue from Egypt. He recalls the language of the book of Exodus, where God saw the "affliction" of his people and came down to deliver them from the hand of the Egyptians (Exod. 3:7–8). So now, says David, God has not abhorred nor despised "the affliction of the afflicted" (that is, David himself), nor has God hidden his face, but instead he has heard David's cry for help.

Reading Exodus 4:31 we witness an automatic response on the part of the Israelites to the news that God had visited "the sons of Israel and that He had seen their affliction": "they bowed low and worshiped" (NASB). Here likewise, David expects the news of his rescue to be greeted by all Israel with worship. Just as the crossing of the Red Sea had prompted a triumphant song accompanied by timbrel and dance, so now David takes up song surrounded by his brothers and sisters in the congregation.

Perhaps it is only natural that Israel's Anointed would invite not just his family members but all the descendants of Jacob and offspring of Israel (v. 23) to celebrate his especially great deliverance. Unexpectedly, though, David goes further and throws the doors open to people from the ends of the earth. Not only do his own family and the covenant faithful have a place at his table of thanks, but so do all the families of the Gentiles (v. 27).

This answers to a whisper in the Hebrew Scriptures that was heard by some but not by all. Mosaic legislation called for God's redeeming love to be reflected in the way Israel provided for strangers, sojourners, and resident aliens (especially Exod. 22:21; 23:9; Lev. 19:33–34). Such "outsiders" within Israel, however, were not just reminders of Israel's past days as aliens in Egypt; they also were a forecast of a great ingathering of the nations. From time to time, the Old Testament gives us a glimpse of Israel's destiny: to unite the human race in peace under the dominion of Yahweh.

These were the terms of the original covenant with Abraham: "And in you all the families of the earth will be blessed" (Gen. 12:3 NASB). They are terms that continue in force beyond David, into the days of Isaiah and even through Malachi, the last of the Hebrew Scriptures' prophets:

> Now it will come about that
> In the last days
> The mountain of the house of the LORD
> Will be established as the chief of the mountains,
> And will be raised above the hills;
> And all the nations will stream to it.
> And many peoples will come and say,
> Come, let us go up to the mountain of the LORD,
> To the house of the God of Jacob.
>
> Isaiah 2:2–3 NASB

> Also the foreigners who join themselves to the LORD,
> To minister to Him, and to love the name of the LORD . . . ;
> Even those I will bring to My holy mountain
> And make them joyful in My house of prayer.
> Their burnt offerings and their sacrifices will be acceptable on
>   My altar;

For My house will be called a house of prayer for all the peoples.

Isaiah 56:6–7 NASB

"For from the rising of the sun even to its setting, My name will be great among the nations, and in every place incense is going to be offered to My name, and a grain offering that is pure; for My name will be great among the nations," says the LORD of hosts.

Malachi 1:11 NASB

The motif of Yahweh's eventual worldwide kingdom and the human race's peaceful unity is beloved by the psalm writers (see especially Psalms 47; 96–98; 117), but it nowhere receives richer and more exuberant anticipation than in Psalm 22. It is hard to imagine that the feast David describes would last but two days! David never saw worship so expansive as this psalm envisions on his earthly pilgrimage, yet he anticipates the day in God's story of redemption when those of the heritage will make room for those from the outside.

The Afflicted and the Fat Ones

To the king's thanksgiving table he invites "the afflicted" or "the humble" (v. 26). The word play in Hebrew is theologically rich. David, he who was once humiliated ('ānî, v. 24), now promises food for the socially humiliated ('ănāwîmm, the same Hebrew term, only now in the plural rather than the singular, v. 26 [v. 27 in the Hebrew]). In welcoming the poor, David shares a concern for—he even wants to transcend—an integral part of Mosaic law. Throughout the Torah, God expects a people who know what it is to be delivered from dispossession to mirror that deliverance by providing relief to the least among them, particularly to aliens, widows, orphans, the needy, and the Levites.[4] David, however, reaches farther than the law's baseline; he provides a lavish feast for the lowly. He wishes eternal life to those whose poverty of soul makes them David's spiritual kin: "Let your heart live forever!" (v. 26 NKJV).

The translators of the Greek Old Testament (the Septuagint) supply a couple of skillful nuances in their rendering of the words that refer to David and his guests. In verse 26 the Septuagint designates those whom David invites to his table with a Greek word usually used for the working poor (Gk., *penēs*): "The (working) poor shall eat and be satisfied." But in verse 24 of the Greek translation, David has already referred to himself as having become worse than that: *ptōchos*, a term normally reserved for the poorest of the poor—the "indigent," beggars and street urchins. For the Anointed One of Israel to number himself among the "indigent" is for him to take the lowliest of social stations.

With David reduced to beggary and now hosting the likes of day laborers, we get a glimpse of what makes Israel's Redeemer-God so distinctive. This God sits high and looks low. The God of Israel stands above any of his human subjects, yet he is rescuer of both the greatest and the least.

Moreover, Israel's working poor are joined at the table of the king's largesse by "all the prosperous of the earth" (v. 29), literally, by "all the fat ones."

Today, when we talk about people who satisfy whatever appetites they have, we say they are "living large." Perhaps the only difference between our society and David's is the percentage of folks who can afford "plus-size" diets. In the ancient world and in many non-Western contemporary societies, the surest way to find a community's elite is to look for "the fat ones." They're the ones whose bodies are not kept lean through labor and the frugal diet that comes with poverty. In many places it is a sign of status not to have to labor or to endure a frugal diet, and the way you display your status is to put on weight.

To be sure, the Scriptures warn against the spiritual peril of satedness.[5] In Psalm 131 David himself says he wants to avoid the pride and haughtiness that befall social elites. This makes it all the more arresting that David welcomes at his table lean and large alike. He brings to his table those whose social and spiritual destitution has prompted them to seek satisfaction in knowing God. He also brings those whose wide girth has not blinded them to the one source of nourishment for their spirit. "You have made my head fat with oil," Israel's shepherd king will acknowledge in Psalm 23:5.[6] The rescued king is pleased to seat rich and poor side by side at his table and to have them both join his hymns of praise to the Father.

Those Who Go Down to the Dust and a People Not Yet Born

We've seen that David's great assembly blurs the boundaries of ethnicity and economics. It also blurs the boundary of time, including the boundary between the living and the dead. The king, no doubt in view of his recent near-death experience ("you have laid me in the dust of death"), calls for worship from "all those who go down to the dust . . . even he who cannot keep his soul alive" (v. 29 NASB).

In Scripture the closely related idiom "to go down to the pit" connotes the awful finality of death. Over and over the psalms beg God: "Do not let me be like those who go down to the pit" (Ps. 28:1). In the death-pit there is no worship. Stuck on this notion, the Sadducees of Jesus's day were confounded at our Lord's claim that a deeper reading of Scripture shows that God relates to his own beyond the grave: the God of Abraham, Isaac, and Jacob "is not the God of the dead but of the living" (Matt. 22:32 NASB). Psalm 22:29 bears one of those hints that prompted Jesus's deeper reading. David promises that those who worship God will discover that death itself will fail to stop their worship.

On the basis of passages like this, and even more on the warrant of Jesus's breaking through the barrier of death in his resurrection, the writer to the Hebrews says that we have come "to the general assembly and church of the firstborn who are enrolled in heaven . . . to the spirits of the righteous made perfect" (Heb. 12:23 NASB). In Christ, the dead and the living make up one community of praise.

Having presented a picture of worship offered by both the living and the dead, David reveals a final group: those who haven't been born yet. The reason he writes this song in the first place is that he wants his experience of God's deliverance to speak to later generations: "It will be told of the Lord to the coming generation" (v. 30 NASB). David understood that whenever any of us comes along in the timeline, and from whatever angle, we are there to serve those who come after us. The yet-to-be are part of our song as well as those who have died in God.

By the end of Psalm 22, David gathers up as vast and as variegated a community of praise as is ever envisioned in the Hebrew Scriptures—Israelite and Gentile, poor and rich, dead and not yet alive. At the center of this gathering, leading a chant of victory is he who at first sang the lament of God's abandonment.

Psalm 22 is a perfect parable of David's worship life. Even when he thinks he is being laid in the dust of death, the Sweet Singer of Israel remembers the aural architecture of the sanctuary: God somehow—mysteriously and sacramentally—resides in the praises of Israel, his people. Instead of swallowing his despair he sings it out to his God. Then he rises from his rescue to sing his great God's praise in the midst of a vast congregation. The result of David's deliverance is that he sings to call a magnificent house of praise into being. This is what makes him the Architect of Praise.

The Singing Savior

Psalm 22 is also a preview of the New Testament's epic of the Messiah's humiliation and glorification. From the cross Jesus will cry, "My God, my God, why have you forsaken me?" David's lament gives perfect expression to the Son of God's agony. At the same time, David's post-deliverance invitation to a celebration sounds the perfect note for what Jesus is going to do after his resurrection: "In the church I will sing hymns to you." The New Testament claims Jesus as Psalm 22's true singer both of the lament of abandonment and of the victory chant.

Early Christians found themselves reading this psalm as a forecast of the sufferings and glory of Jesus Christ. The Savior himself alluded to Psalm 22 in his own agonized cry from the cross. Even though none of the Gospel accounts uses the specific language of "pierced" hands and feet, Jesus's quoting of the first line of the psalm while his own wrists and ankles were pierced with nails opened this psalm up to his followers.

Indeed, when they examined the text, Gospel writers—especially Matthew and Mark—found that the details of the crucifixion had already been laid out a thousand years beforehand. In light of the death of their Savior, they could not help but read crucifixion's slow suffocation in David's words about his being poured out like water, about his bones being out of joint, and about his heart melting like wax. Having witnessed soldiers gambling for Jesus's garments and having heard the crowd taunting him, the Gospel writers must have been awestruck that God had written such unwitting players into the text of his drama of redemption.

Along with all the other writers of the New Testament, Matthew and Mark understood that their suffering Savior was David's greater Son and thus Israel's true "Sweet Singer." They understood that his exile of abandonment on the cross had won their acceptance and that his bitter song of lament had been the price of the forgiveness of their sins. They believed that the first two-thirds of Psalm 22 had been a straightforward prophecy of the means of their redemption through the cross.

Early Christians further understood that the last third of this psalm was about their Savior. They knew that because of Christ's death and resurrection, "the kingdom is the LORD's and He rules over the nations" (Ps. 22:28 NASB). This meant the afflicted would eat and be satisfied, the ends of the earth would remember and turn to the Lord, and all the families of the nations would worship. They knew Christ's resurrection meant that death was not the end of fellowship between God and his children, and they knew they had an incredible story of redemption to pass on to their children and their children's children.

The writer to the Hebrews summed it up when he placed upon the ascended Jesus's lips the words of Psalm 22:22 as a prayer to his Father:

> I will tell of your name to my brethren;
> In the midst of the assembly I will sing hymns to you.
>
> Hebrews 2:12

In this passage Jesus takes his place in God's great "assembly," a word that both in the Greek translation of Psalm 22 and in the original Greek of Hebrews 2:12 is *ekklēsia*, or "church." In the church Jesus is chief liturgist or worship leader, both declaring the Father's name and singing his praises.

The writer to the Hebrews thus recognizes that by virtue of his resurrection and ascension Jesus has become the Architect of Praise, Lord over a house of flesh and blood that God is building where he inhabits his people's praise. While Moses had been faithful, says the writer, *in* the house, Jesus the apostle, high priest, and builder of the house, is faithful *over* the house, "whose house we are, if we hold fast our endurance and the boast of our hope firm to the end" (Heb. 3:6).

As builder and head over the house of God's dwelling, Jesus stands as "mediator of a new covenant" in the midst of "the general assembly" of a church united in heaven and on earth. There he leads our "sacrifice of praise to God, that is, the fruit of lips that give thanks to His name" (Heb. 12:23–24; 13:15 NASB).

In a sense Psalm 22 is the theological center of the book of Psalms. Like Israel's pilgrimage it begins in loneliness and dejection and ends, on the far side of God's miraculous intervention, in comradeship and elation. With its "My God, my God" and its "I will sing hymns," Psalm 22 makes the whole of the biblical drama present to us. If the Bible is about utter lostness getting turned around, Psalm 22 tells that story about as compactly and emotively as can be done. Here David takes us as low as he ever goes ("I am a worm and not a man," v. 6) and as high ("From You comes my praise in the great assembly," v. 25 NASB). In David's traversing the whole range of human possibilities, we get a view into the whole range of Israel's experience, and we find words for our own experiences.

Moreover, Psalm 22 is the musical bridge between Israel's greatest king and humankind's King of Kings. In this psalm we hear a thousand years ahead of time the singular Voice that sings us all from shame to glory. Thus Psalm 22 is the hinge in our theology of song.

5

Jesus's Lament
of Abandonment

One scenario of death truly scares me: sliding into Alzheimer's disease, gradually losing mental capacity, shedding layer after layer of self-constructing memory, until only body functions are left. My father recently died of this disease. It was excruciating to watch this retired college professor—a man who defined himself by means of his thoughts and his memories—lose that which had always made his life worth living.

Shortly before his death, my father shared a room with another Alzheimer's patient. Had I met Mr. Couch pre-Alzheimer's, I know I would have found him easy to like. He is a retired pharmacist and a former stamp collector. According to his nurses, he was once an ebullient and sparkling conversationalist. Now he is only occasionally conversant. When he does talk, it is clear he is aware enough of what is happening to him that it hurts.

Sometimes, though, Mr. Couch betrays an unmistakable cheerfulness. One night, while my family and I were visiting my father, Mr. Couch lay in his bed, sleeping restlessly. I watched for a moment, wishing another end for him, as well as for my father and, beyond that, praying for a different end for myself. All of a sudden, still asleep, Mr. Couch began singing:

> Abide with me: fast falls the eventide.
> The darkness deepens; Lord, with me abide.
> When other helpers fail, and comforts flee,
> Help of the helpless, O abide with me.

I found myself wondering, could this unconsciously raised hymn tell the tale of a sadness not borne alone? Could there be something more to Mr. Couch's occasional cheerfulness? Despite the deepening darkness of Alzheimer's, could he who is the "Help of the helpless" be abiding in the depths of the man lying before me?

The Lament of the Singing Savior

He hung alone.

Well, not completely alone.

There were the would-be revolutionaries on either side, one a scoffer, the other a new friend, each encased in his own cocoon of pain.

There were the three Marys, his own mother among them. At least one follower was there as well, the one whom he specially loved and entrusted with his mother's care.

Of course, there were also the soldiers, doctors of pain and humiliation, who, just as Psalm 22:18 had prophesied, shot craps to see who would get the last of his clothes.

Finally, there was the crowd. They were Psalm 22:16's congregation of evildoers, as spiteful and demented as forecast, wagging their heads and hurling abuse, their leaders (no doubt unknowingly, and considering their training in Scripture, inexcusably) taking up the mantra David had predicted ten centuries earlier: "He trusts in God. Let God rescue him now if he wants him" (Matt. 27:43 NIV).

Ironically, then, he was not completely alone. Still, at a more fundamental level, he was left desolate by the One whose presence truly mattered: "My God, my God, why have you forsaken me?" Using the opening words of Psalm 22, God's Son lifts a bitter dirge of forsakenness to a Father who promised he would never abandon his own. He who knew the Father's voice from eternity and was the author of sound for all creation heard nothing but silence. With the cry, in the unforgettable words of G. K. Chesterton, "God seemed for an instant to be an atheist."[1]

Yet Christians confess that, quite contrary to appearances, this is the moment God became believable. The tearing of the flesh of Jesus was the ripping of the curtain between God and us, as Matthew says, from top to bottom (27:51). In Jesus's suffering visage, God showed his face. On the cross God took our side.

In this chapter we consider Jesus's song of exile, in the next his song of enthronement. David's mournful songs prefigured Jesus's lonely cry from the cross. Jesus's lament is the vivid culmination of all the pain Israel had ever known and that any of us will ever experience. Jesus's lament is the full expression of human suffering. It is our lament.

We all know the loneliness of exile, whether because of fractured relationships, unfulfilled expectations, or bitter and hurtful words we can't unsay. Christ's wounded cry is healing because it means we do not suffer alone.

Into Exile: The Silent Treatment

When God delivered his song of testimony to Moses, he said he would hide his face in the day of Israel's rebellion (Deut. 31:18). Each year the sins of God's people were symbolically placed on a goat, and the goat was turned out of the city into the wilderness to die. This was a picture of the removal of sin from the presence of God. Either the sinner goes, or the goat (Lev. 16).

The Bible portrays the converse, too. The prophet Ezekiel pictures God removing himself from a sinful people's presence. In Ezekiel 10, God leaves the temple, so the glory cloud leaves the city. All that's left in the wake of God's departure is spiritual death. That's why it's to a valley of "dry bones" that Ezekiel brings the message of restoration at the end of the book: "Son of man, these bones are the whole house of Israel" (Ezek. 37:11 NASB).

On the first Good Friday, God carried out the threat he had issued through Moses: he hid his face at his people's rebellion. The God of glory drew back from sin's presence and left true Israel desolate and dying on a cross.

It was not from his people in the aggregate that God turned away; it was from his people embodied in his Son. David's first singing of "My God, my God, why have you forsaken me?" turns out to have been a premonition of a day when a Favored Son would watch his Father desert him. What darkened the sky that day was God's refusal to save the only Israelite who never rebelled. This lonely death was the exile of which all of Israel's captivities were mere warnings. Ezekiel's horrifying threat that God would leave a valley of "dry bones" when he withdrew his glory cloud received macabre embodiment as the one loyal child of the covenant cried out in abandonment and was laid in the dust of death.

Surely, even when David composed Psalm 22, he knew his incredulity at being ignored by God was at least somewhat inflated. His innocence was relative. We've seen his acknowledgment in other psalms that he was a sinner in need of forgiveness (e.g., Psalms 32; 51). By contrast, Jesus, the true Singer of this psalm, was "without sin." When he protests his abandonment, he does it with grounds. But by some divine arrangement Jesus took the cross to become the reality of what all those annual scapegoats merely pictured: he became sin and was cursed by God, says Paul (2 Cor. 5:21; Gal. 3:13).

The sending away that had been merely figured in the scapegoats became flesh and blood on the day Jesus suffered "outside the gate" (Heb. 13:12). Literally, his Roman cross was placed outside the gates of the city of Jerusalem. More to the point, his was a death at the hands of pagans; and it was death by hanging on a tree, which in the Old Testament brought the ultimate in divine rejection: "cursed is every one who is hanged on a tree" (Deut. 21:23). Even if they had been trying, the Romans could not have invented a form of execution better to max out the Old Testament's meter of shame. Spiritually, by means of his crucifixion "outside the gate," Jesus took our sins out into the wilderness of damnation.

Polite Romans did not utter the term *crucifixion*. Rather, at least according to Cicero, they referred to it with the euphemism: "hanging on the unlucky tree." Victims of "the unlucky tree" were stripped naked and their crosses were strategically placed alongside public thoroughfares. Exposure was the point—baring of skin to show contemptibility of soul. Psalm 22 anticipates the feeling, "I am a worm and not a man" (v. 22). In another psalm as well, David anticipates the shame of Jesus's cross:

> Those who sit in the gate talk about me,
> And I am the song of the drunkards . . .
> They also gave me gall for my food
> And for my thirst they gave me vinegar.
>
> Psalm 69:12, 21 NASB

While he nakedly sang his agony, they brazenly sang their mockery. This is why the writer to the Hebrews says Jesus despised the shame of the cross (Heb. 12:2). Jesus's nakedness on the cross is an unveiling of the ugliness of our inner souls. There, he takes on a spiritual disfigurement that is necessary if he is to reclaim us from beastliness. He hung as God's ugly fool—the butt of his executioners' cruel humor.

Yet he sings. We've already noticed how David could not help but sing to God even when he felt God had turned away from him. We've seen that it was impossible for Israel to respond to being exiled outside the Promised Land without singing about hanging their harps on the willows by the Euphrates. Now, Jesus, feeling the presence of the Father being withdrawn from him, calls up one of the laments David bequeathed to Israel. To know the God who is, is to look to him even when he won't make eye contact. To know the God who keeps covenant is to sing to him, even, perhaps especially, when you fear he may not be listening. On the cross, God's Son sings his loathing of what he had to become for us. Nonetheless, he sings.

Once, the great Jewish scholar Emil Fackenheim tried to explain why Jews can believe themselves to be part of God's good purposes even after Auschwitz. He said "midrashic stubbornness" persuades people that once God has written them into his story, he won't write them out of it. On the cross, despite Chesterton's epigram about God's atheism, a Son sings with "midrashic stubbornness." He cannot resist believing his abandonment is part of a greater, victorious story.

In that story Jesus's rejection becomes our acceptance, his cursedness our forgiveness, his nakedness our covering, his ugliness our beauty.

Songs of "The Fellowship of His Sufferings"

Christians believe God raised Jesus from the dead, showing his full satisfaction with Jesus's sacrifice for our sins. The song

of resurrection is what we'll explore in the next chapter. But here
we want to consider what Jesus's song of death continues to mean
for us. We will never have to sing "My God, my God, why have
you forsaken me" the way he did. But we still experience forsakenness and loneliness. We will not have to taste damnation the
way he did, but our bodies still decay and we die while we wait
for resurrection. We have been forgiven, but we still mess up. In
all this, Jesus's song of suffering sustains us.

According to G. K. Chesterton, what makes Christianity such
an adventurous project is its wild extremes: the sorrow of the
cross and the joy of the empty tomb. Chesterton calls this "the
romance of orthodoxy."[2] Christianity is not about a bland "middle ground," stuck somewhere between high and low. It is not a
canceling of cold and hot. Knowing Christ is about embracing
what the apostle Paul calls "the power of His resurrection and
the fellowship of His sufferings" (Phil. 3:10 NASB). Many of us
with stoicism seek simply to cope with life. We paint our canvas
in safe, if bland, grays. But real Christianity surrounds us with
the reddest reds and the bluest blues, the bleakest blacks and the
most radiant whites. It is not about mere resignation and coping
mechanisms. It is about resurrection and crucifixion, triumph
and failure, redemption and sin.

The cross is our way through exile, through abandonment,
through the shame of our nakedness, through the contemptibility
of our souls. The cross brings with it a realization of a joy we can
know only in sorrow and a beauty we can find only in the ugly.
The cross, therefore, calls forth "hymns that know the fellowship
of His sufferings, hymns that can come from a cross, or rise from
a prison cell at midnight," says Ed Clowney.[3]

The cross brings God into deep places in our lives—places
where artists, poets, and musicians go. Right around the time
my pastor, Mort Whitman, took me to Handel's *Messiah*, he introduced me to the art of Georges Rouault, thought by many to

be "the greatest religious artist since Rembrandt."[4] Stained-glass apprentice and companion of the early twentieth-century artists known as *Les Fauves* ("The Beasts"), Rouault developed the unusual capacity to paint the depths of human ugliness redemptively. Rouault's visages of Christ are timelessly iconic and yet perfectly matched to his own world of sorrowful clowns, angry prostitutes, proud kings, and imperious judges.

In a panel from Rouault's most famous work, *Miserere*, a slain soldier is borne aloft by an angel. Above the soldier's family, gathered around him in grief, hangs a portrait of Christ, suffering yet radiating light. Beneath, Rouault has inscribed, "The just, like sandalwood, perfume the axe that strikes them."[5]

A dear friend and fellow worship leader lost a son to drowning. Hers was an unimaginably excruciating loss. But all you have to do is listen to her pray to know what Rouault means. And when she sings, there's a loveliness that comes from somewhere beyond her giftedness and training. It is the aroma of sandalwood. Somehow her loss has made Christ more present to her. Somewhere deep inside us we all know we are fragile, but it's not until we can see our fragility in the thorn-crowned countenance of Jesus that we can face it.

Praise be to God, we have wonderful music that probes the depths of Christ's humiliation and suffering. His death has occasioned some of the most compelling and beautiful music the West has ever produced. The voices range from classical to folk to popular. Bach told the story of the passion from the apostle John's perspective in an eighteenth-century classical idiom; Arvo Pärt retold it in a twentieth-century classical way. We have spirituals such as "Were You There?"; older hymn tunes such as Lowell Mason's setting of "When I Survey the Wondrous Cross"; and newer settings for older hymns such as Eric Ashley's "O Come and Mourn with Me Awhile." Contemporary composers press the musical language of popular culture into the service of the passion story; I mention only Steve Hindalong's "Beautiful, Scandalous Night"; Mark Altrogge's "We Sing Your Mercies"; and Graham Kendrick's "Servant King." Remembering Jesus's death in song helps us take our place in what Paul calls "the fellowship of his sufferings."

For a number of years a local church has offered a lunch-hour Good Friday service that consists of simple readings of the "Seven Words from the Cross" interwoven with songs and hymns that linger on those beautifully tragic, redemptive moments. This service is the high point of my personal liturgical calendar. Two songs that are not well known but that are often included in the service are William Billings's haunting round "When Jesus Wept" and Dan Schutte's eerie "Holy Darkness."

Billings is sometimes referred to as America's original composer. By the end of the late eighteenth century, many New England pastors were urging a reform in music because oral tradition had failed to preserve the music of psalm singing. At the call of the pastors, "singing masters" established "singing schools" to raise musical literacy in the churches and to restore congregational song. Preeminent among these masters was Billings. His round "By the Waters of Babylon" (based on Psalm 137) is well known, by virtue of its appearing on Don McLean's *American Pie* album of 1971. "When Jesus Wept" is that song's New Testament counterpart:

> When Jesus wept, the falling tear in mercy flowed beyond all bound.
> When Jesus groaned, a trembling fear seized all the guilty world around.[6]

The way William Schuman incorporates Billings's melody into the second movement of his own *New England Triptych* is wrenchingly lovely.[7] But there's nothing more lovely than a congregation singing it as a canon on Good Friday.

Dan Schutte, formerly of the folk group St. Louis Jesuits, based his "Holy Darkness" on a text by the Spanish medieval mystic, St. John of the Cross. I can almost hear the Father singing to the Son in the Garden of Gethsemane:

> I have tried you in fires of affliction; I have taught your soul to grieve.
> In the barren soil of your loneliness, there will I plant my seed.
>
> I have taught the price of compassion; you have stood before the grave.
> Though my love can seem like a raging storm, this is the love that saves.
>
> In your deepest hour of darkness I will give you wealth untold.
> When the silence stills your spirit, will my riches fill your soul.

And though the chorus is expressed in the first person plural and is sung by the congregation, I cannot help but hear in it the Son of God's final "yes" to the abandonment that would bring the salvation of the world:

> Holy darkness, blessed night, heaven's answer hidden from our sight.
> As we await you, O God of silence, we embrace your holy night.[8]

One of those Good Fridays a few years ago, the service's music stayed with me all afternoon. "When Jesus Wept" and "Holy Darkness" rolled through my mind over and over again. The wonder of Christ's death clung to me. I was so much more aware than I would have been otherwise of what a beautiful spring afternoon it was. The sky was a resplendent blue, and the cumulus clouds were piled to the heavens. The groan of two thousand years ago, by which "a trembling fear seized all the guilty world around," hit the harmonics of my soul and drew from somewhere deep within a groan of awe that I should be a participant in this death and its effects.

That afternoon, at rush hour, my car broke down at a busy intersection. Uncharacteristically, I was not put out. I decided to sit next to my car for a while and watch people drive by. I wondered about their stories. I read their bumper stickers for clues as to their passions and pains, and I prayed for them accordingly. The next thing I knew, a friend and rival Little League coach pulled up and offered help, making him late, it turns out, for his team's practice. A little thing. The sort of thing that happens all the time. But I had heard old words newly that day ("Father, forgive them") and had sung songs that made Jesus's sufferings a living presence. I felt I had been allowed to touch something solid beneath the ephemera of day-to-day living.

Christ's death-song makes reality more real. It squashes fears, pulls us out of our self-absorption, and connects us to others. Songs that keep Christ's death before us help us in another way: they help us acknowledge how messed up we are. That's a good thing. It's the cross that frees Rouault, in another panel from the *Miserere*, to do a self-portrait as a sad clown and to inscribe beneath it: "Do we not all paint our faces?" We know we are base, but we cannot name our baseness until we see it borne for us. Once we see Christ as bearer of our foolishness, though, we gain the freedom to let go of our pretense—self-made happiness, self-painted beauty, self-generated dignity, self-defined rightness.

Among the apostles, Paul is unrivaled in his insight into the way the cross redefines self-understanding. No one knows better the freedom from self-delusion that comes with the forgiveness of sins: "I know that nothing good dwells in me, that is, in my flesh. I can will what is right, but I cannot do it" (Rom. 7:18). Paul shows us a personal candor greater even than David's. For the

first time in the history of religion, says New Testament scholar
Gerd Theissen, we find a person admitting that despite his own
consciousness of not being at fault in a matter, he may be quite in
error: "I am conscious of nothing against myself, yet I am not by
this acquitted" (1 Cor. 4:4 NASB). However, Paul believes it doesn't
matter, because it has been covered. As a result, no one is bolder
in allowing the cross to redefine his self-understanding.[9] In the
chronology of his writings, Paul begins as "least of the apostles,"
demotes himself to "least of the saints," and finally puts himself at
the end of the line as "chief of sinners."[10] We are, he says, "under
sentence of death" (1 Cor. 4:9). No one understands better how
we may see Christ's death as ours and our lives as a constant
dying in Christ.

Paul expects us to govern our lives in view of the truth he
stated in addressing the church at Colossae: "You have died
and your life is hidden with Christ in God" (Col. 3:3 NASB).
He is keenly aware how radical it is for us to imagine ourselves
in this way. That's why he's so urgent in commending song as
a way to know the richness of Christ in his word (Col. 3:16).
The result for him personally is a rich musical imagination, one
that lets him appeal to a "noisy gong," a "clanging cymbal," an
"indistinctly" played harp or flute, and an "unclearly" played
trumpet to describe loveless and unedifying speech (1 Cor.
13:1; 14:7–9). More, Paul knows how to bring his innermost
fears and frustrations to God through song. We find him singing psalms in a Philippian jail cell in the middle of the night
(Acts 16:25).

Acknowledging Our Hurts

Some time back I was consumed with anger. I was mad about
work. I was mad about my father's Alzheimer's. I was mad about
things in my personality that I couldn't change. I was even mad

about the way I perceived I was being treated by my local Little League. It so happened that this all came to a head during a two-week period when my schedule had left me with some time for contemplation.

I found myself meditating on a single phrase in Paul's letter to the Galatians: "I am crucified with Christ" (2:20). The text was pressed upon me as I watched a miracle of grace take place in my father's life. He caught pneumonia about the time I was going into my funk of anger, and one night at the hospital his physician told me he didn't expect my dad to last till morning. That night, the mental fog lifted just long enough for my father to cry out in childlike faith for the first time in his life: "God, I want you in my life." Instead of expiring, he began to mend. By morning it was clear he would survive. His confusion returned, but he was a different man.

Before that night, I had been watching my father die alone and bitter. Afterwards, not so. I felt as if I had been given a rare privilege: watching Christ come to someone's side and take his death upon himself. I found it harder to feel sorry for myself. My father was given two more years with us, and of all his ninety-one years, they were the most relaxed, contented, and thankful. He was no longer alone. Neither was I.

During these two weeks of contemplation I immersed myself in Rouault's *Miserere* and in one of his lesser known works, *The Passion*, a series of vividly colored plates that accompany a poem by his friend Andres Suares about Christ's crucifixion. I soaked in Rouault's juxtaposition of Christ's humiliation and the human race's brokenness. As I did so, I listened over and over again to three pieces of music. The first was Henryk Gorecki's *Miserere*, a thirty-two-minute choral meditation on five simple words, *Domine Deus noster, Miserere nobis* ("Lord our God, have mercy on us"). The second was Ralph Vaughan Williams's orchestral piece *Fantasia on a Theme by Thomas Tallis*. Tallis had written his theme in the sixteenth century as accompaniment for

Psalm 2: "Why do the nations conspire and the peoples plot in vain?" Its evocative modality drove home to me the horror and scandal of the crucifixion.

The third piece of music was "Surely God Is with Us," a song the Ragamuffin Band recorded to honor their leader Rich Mullins, who had planned to record the song on his *Jesus Record* before he was killed in an automobile accident in 1997. The song is a folk rock anthem to Christ's coming to make a kingdom of "paupers, simpletons and rogues. The whores all seem to love Him and the drunks propose a toast: 'Surely God is with us.'"[11]

I needed Gorecki to make me sit for a half hour at a time imploring forgiveness. I needed Vaughan Williams to turn my sense of tonality inside out and make me admit that I too "rage" and "fume" against my Maker. I needed the Ragamuffins to name me among the vagabonds my Lord had come to reclaim.

Between the power of Paul's words, the miracle God was working in my father, the concreteness with which Rouault depicted Christ coming into my world, and the three composers' relentless penitence, a divine alchemy was at work. I found myself shedding the anger and embracing a Savior who had come into my darkness.

Life is hard. That's why so many of the psalms are laments. That's why so many hymns of previous eras dealt with death: "Rock of Ages" ("when mine eyelids close in death"), "Be Still, My Soul" ("when dearest friends depart, and all is darkened in the vale of tears"), "Jesus, I Live to Thee" ("Jesus, I die to thee, whenever death shall come"), and "Guide Me, O Thou Great Jehovah":

> When I tread the verge of Jordan,
> Bid my anxious fears subside;
> Death of death and hell's Destruction,
> Land me safe on Canaan's side.
> Songs of praises, songs of praises
> I will ever give to thee,
> I will ever give to thee.

No matter how hard we try to insulate ourselves from life's harshness, it forces itself upon us. Loved ones die. Friends betray. Dreams fade. World and national events compel us to confess that evil and hatred are strong. Names like The Murrah Building, Columbine High School, and the World Trade Center have given us a new lexicon of horror. But they also have given us moments of insight into the way that music can touch us in our grief. The nationally televised memorial service in Oklahoma City was graced by violinist/fiddler Mark O'Connor's rendering of "Amazing Grace." No small part of the healing in Littleton, Colorado, was a song by two brothers, Stephen and Jonathan Cohen, who were on campus the day of the shootings: "In God's son, hope will come, his red stain will take our pain. Columbine, friend of mine."[12]

We have songs that let us know the suffering side of our Savior better. We have songs that open us up to our own sinfulness. The cross, moreover, offers a perspective that helps us live more realistically with the consequences of the fall. Our redemption has a "not yet" side to it; that is to say, we're not all the way home just yet. Music has a way of sobering us up to that fact.

Living with the Fall

William "Pappy" Fehr, longtime conductor of the choir at the College of William and Mary, is reported to have replied once to a would-be flatterer, "No, ma'am, I don't think God was pleased with that concert. You see, He has perfect pitch." The lesson is that in a fallen world, there is no such thing as perfection. In some churches the quest for "excellence" is an idol, regardless of whether "excellence" is defined by standards of so-called "classical" culture or of "pop" culture. Such "excellentism" needs to be replaced with the quest to pursue the likeness of Christ crucified and him alone. As good as it gets this side of Christ's return, we're never going to get it completely right. There will always be a flat tenor, a broken guitar string, an overly loud organ, or a poorly placed hymn. But it's okay. The cross means it's covered. That realization will free us from putting one another under a bondage we're not meant to have. It will free us to take some risks and make our worship environments places where it's safe to be grace-needy folks.

The idol of "excellentism" died a glorious death for me one Sunday in church. The soloist that day sang off pitch and with a quaky, amateurish voice. It wasn't all nerves, either: she just wasn't a very good singer. She was offering "So His Honor," a bluesy lament by composer James Ward based on Philippians 1:21–24. The song is a prayer for the boldness to live in such a way that whether the singer lives or dies, Christ's "honor may be seen in my body."[13]

Though the singing was not pretty, nobody noticed. Most people there knew how hard this dear sister in Christ fought just to get out of bed every morning. Her bouts of depression and her battle with an eating disorder made her nearly suicidal. What we all heard that day was a courageous confession that she would stay in the fight, so that, live or die, Christ would be honored in her body. I don't think God's perfect pitch was offended.

From the perspective of the New Testament writers, we are all, just as this sister, in the process of being molded to bear Christ's likeness. It hurts. "Always pain before the child is born . . . Why the dark before the dawn?" sings Bono.[14] It is redemptive hurt, to be sure, for it is, in Paul's terms, a being crucified *with Christ* (Gal. 2:20). But it is crucifixion nonetheless, and so it hurts. We too find ourselves being laid in the dust of death (Ps. 22:5). Perhaps we will lament as orphans or, perhaps worse, as spoiled whiners. But we can choose to lament as sons and daughters who know they are loved and are therefore being disciplined and shaped. The difference will lie largely in learning to suffer to the tune of the Savior's song.

6

JESUS'S VICTORY CHANT

I nearly lost a son to drowning. It happened over ten years ago, but it feels like yesterday. "I can't tell you how nice it is for one of these stories to have a happy ending," one of the police officers told us afterwards. "They usually don't." Because my son survived, his bedroom isn't a shrine; it's a place where a teenager lives. I couldn't be more grateful for the pile of dirty clothes on the floor each day. Everything about my relationship with my son is different because he is alive. I'm not nurturing a memory but dealing with a living presence. We play the guitar together, practice baseball together, pray together; we even study Greek together. My life is entwined with his, now and as far into the future as either of us can see.

Jesus's Story Continues

"It makes a big difference whether we think someone is dead or alive," begins New Testament scholar Luke Timothy Johnson's book, *Living Jesus.*[1] If we think Jesus of Nazareth is dead, Johnson contends, we will take up tools appropriate to a quest to learn about a person whose life is confined to the remote past. Into our "tool kits" we'll put lexicons, maps, and scholarly journals. If, however, we think Jesus is still alive, we will have to ask what other tools we'll need. We'll be open to learning *from* and not merely *about* him. We'll have to entertain the possibility that a quest without worship, prayer, and obedience will lead nowhere.

> This seems to be one of those very few choices that allow no equivocation. There is no middle ground between dead and alive. If Jesus is dead, then his story is completed. If he is alive, then his story continues.[2]

Johnson's book is a trenchant and welcome call to his colleagues in New Testament academia to rethink the assumptions they bring to their work. But he could just as well be writing to the church about the way it worships. Our worship can be predicated on one of the same two assumptions. If Jesus is dead, why worship him? If he's alive, our worship is part of the continuation of his story.

Jesus said he would come back from the dead. Still, when he did, he seems to have caught everyone, friend and foe alike, by surprise. Just as people were adjusting to his absence, he was back. Incredible as it is, though, the bare *fact* that he came back is less amazing than what that fact *means.* Breaking death's boundary wasn't entirely new to him, after all: he had already returned a daughter to her parents, a son to his mother, a friend to his sisters.[3] In each instance, though, he had merely pushed back the rule of death. He had resuscitated corpses and extended lives for a season. His own return from the dead was different.

Though Jesus "was crucified in weakness," says Paul, he now "lives by the power of God" (2 Cor. 13:4 NKJV). Jesus came back from the dead empowered to do two things: undo Adam's mess and build David's house. The risen Jesus is the "Last Adam" because he passed the test that the first Adam failed. Jesus returned from the dead to sing the walking dead back to life. Further, the risen Jesus is the true heir of David. He returned to build a better temple than David's first heir did, not a building that *houses* people singing but a building that *is* people singing.

The first Adam's rebellion dragged all his sons and daughters into a quagmire of sin, moral impotence, and beastliness. Jesus's obedience and death break the curse on Adam's sons and daughters. With his resurrection Jesus becomes, as Paul says, a "life-giving spirit" (1 Cor. 15:45): he breaks sin's hold, he breathes life into corpses, he makes us human again. "If any one is in Christ, there is new creation," says Paul (2 Cor. 5:17).

Paul Learns the Power of the Resurrection

Paul could write about a new creation because he experienced this himself. Before his conversion, he was doing fine—more than fine. His was a life of privilege, passion, and purpose. He was born into one of Israel's noblest family lines, he was fortunate enough to be born with a triple citizenship (Roman, Tarsian, and Hebrew), and he had the benefit of the finest education his heritage had to offer. He claims that he was zealous for "the traditions of the fathers," that he was, in fact, unsurpassed among his contemporaries in his zeal. He means by this that he was a dedicated partisan of the Pharisee party. He aggressively worked to purify God's people of personal and social pollution in anticipation of the day of God's visitation, Israel's vindication in the eyes of the nations, and the resurrection of the faithful to everlasting life.

When Paul persecuted early believers, he was on a mission he thought was from God. How could a dead Messiah do anybody any good? The claim that resurrection had taken place before the end of the world was absurd. There is nothing in his writings or in Luke's recollections of his career to indicate Paul had a hint of self-doubt or guilty conscience before his encounter with Christ on the road to Damascus in Syria. On hindsight, he maintained he was as dead as the most lost Gentile: "And so we were by nature children of wrath, like the rest of mankind" (Eph. 2:3 RSV). In later letters to Timothy and Titus he leaves the impression that underlying his zeal had been pride, malice, and lovelessness (1 Tim. 1:13; Titus 3:3).

When Jesus spoke his own name to Paul beyond the grave—"It is I Jesus, whom you are persecuting"—life for Paul started all over again. His friend Luke would later describe it in terms of something like scales falling off his eyes so he could see again (Acts 9:5, 18). In the first place, of course, that has to do with the fact that Paul was temporarily blinded by the light that struck him down. But there's more to it: when he realized that Christ was no longer among the dead, Paul came to see everything in a new way. He saw that the world to come could not be entered into by anyone without the saving death of God's own Son. The cost of his redemption made him recalculate how much his own covenant faithfulness had been worth: absolutely nothing. Now alive to a God whose mercy and grace had become flesh and blood rather than abstract theological concepts, Paul allowed himself to be baptized, thus signifying that he was taking his own place in the death and resurrection of Jesus.

Especially amazing is the rechanneling of Paul's zealotry, and there's no better indicator of this aspect of his conversion than the fact that he now knows a *Singing* Savior. Throughout his letter to the Christians of Rome, Paul addresses a spirit of antagonism that has emerged between Jewish and Gentile segments in that city.[4] Paul warns Gentile Christians about adopting either an arrogant attitude toward non-Christian Jews (11:18) or a condescending attitude toward overly scrupulous Christian Jews (chapter 14). He wants Gentile and Jewish Christians to accept one another, and more: he wants them "together with one voice to glorify the God and Father of our Lord Jesus Christ" (15:6). He reminds them that Jesus has become servant of both Jew and Gentile. To spark their united praise he points to Jesus, who, Paul says, is singing among the nations:

> I will praise you among the Gentiles;
> and sing to your name.[5]

This converted Pharisee thinks of the church's evangelism as Jesus singing among the nations, drawing Gentiles and Jews together so they might offer a chorus of praise to the Father. Through Paul's own mission, he hears Jesus *singing* nations into submission by singing them into *life*. Paul takes the idea from Psalm 18, a psalm we noted earlier by which David celebrates his deliverance from his pursuers. No longer a fugitive from Saul, David saw himself enthroned as chief missionary of Israel to the nations. In Paul's view, now Jesus has risen as scion of David—Israel's true "Sweet Singer"—to take Israel's song of redemption to the nations. Jewish and Gentile believers are under a weighty obligation to join a united voice to their Singing Savior's. Just as Jesus sings love where there was once estrangement, so must his followers. Displacing the sort of indignation that had originally sent a pre-Christian Paul to Damascus to punish Jesus's followers for exporting their "heresy" to the nation of Syria, there is now a sweetness of spirit—a desire to showcase God's reconciling power to make Jews and Gentiles one in the risen Messiah. It is the *singing* side of Jesus that redeems Paul's zealotry and transforms it into loving, life-giving ardor.

Seeing Jesus in a Different Light

To understand Jesus to be the kind of Singing Savior Paul imagines him to be is to see him in a whole new light. My first job out of seminary was as an assistant pastor. I served a church in which Christian counselor Larry Crabb was an elder. He had just published his first two books on counseling, challenging churches to become places where struggling believers can find help. As one of the elders, he added his wisdom to the direction of the church's ministry. As teacher, preacher, advisor, and counselor, Larry showed a penetrating grasp of the pain with which most people live.

For all that, though, the most enduring image I have of Larry is of his leading singing for our Sunday evening services. He delighted in simple praise choruses and testimony songs. His enthusiasm was contagious. He had a distinctive way of conducting the congregation's singing. His arm didn't follow a standard choral director's pattern. Instead, Larry moved his arm more intuitively: his arm went up and down with the notes of the melody and from side to side pulsing with the beat of the song. Somehow his arm took us where the music was going. Larry would expand the last line of the chorus "He Lives," leading with his strong tenor voice:

> You ask me how I know he lives:
> He lives (dramatic pause, arm high in the air),
> he lives (dramatic pause, arm higher),
> he lives (dramatic pause, arm as high as it could go)
> within my heart!

To appreciate all that Larry Crabb offers the church, you have to see him as more than a thoughtful writer, a profound teacher and preacher, and a preeminent counselor. You have to picture him as a joyous, arm-waving leader of praise. This role informs everything else. His counsel penetrates. His worship radiates. But in fact the counsel depends on the worship. His obvious joy at singing of his great Redeemer makes you see with a fresh perspective his wrestling with the sober aspects of Christian living.

Grace has kissed him, and he is in relentless pursuit of its power to remake spirits crushed by the curse of sin.

Jesus is like that. It's only when we understand his presence in the church as being the fulfillment of God's promise in Zephaniah 3:17 (NIV) to "quiet you with his love" and "rejoice over you with singing" that a crucial aspect of our salvation comes into perspective. Jesus didn't coldly settle accounts for us. He doesn't bark us into improving ourselves. He unites us to himself in the glorious communion he has enjoyed for eternity with his heavenly Father. He resides within us to heal the broken places and reflesh cauterized hearts. He sings us into a new mode of existence. When we respond to his singing over us, we understand what kind of a king it is who has come to reclaim God's dominion. When, as Paul does, we imagine Jesus *singing* nations into submission to his rule, our hearts come joyfully under the sway of a love that is infinite and powerful. We become that much more alive:

> He speaks and, listening to his voice,
> New life the dead receive;
> The mournful, broken hearts rejoice;
> The humble poor believe.
>
> Hear him, ye deaf; his praise, ye dumb,
> Your loosened tongues employ;
> Ye blind, behold your Savior come;
> And leap, ye lame, for joy.[6]

Why the New Testament Sings

It should come as no surprise that parts of the New Testament take on a songlike quality. It's almost as if its writers are helping the church take up her part in Christ's song. Paul's theology, for instance, drifts toward the poetic and hymnic in the latter half of his writing ministry when, ironically, he does most of his writing from prison.[7] We have noted the way Luke portrays Paul singing hymns in prison in Philippi the very first time his proclamation of Christ gets him arrested (Acts 16:25). To those same Philippians he writes ten years later, once again in jail, this time apparently in Rome where he awaits an audience with the emperor Nero. In phraseology that reads like an anthem, Paul rehearses the pattern of Christ's sufferings and exaltation:

> Who, being in the form of God
> did not regard as grasping
> being equal with God,
> But emptied himself,
>   the form of a slave taking,
> in likeness of men becoming;
> And in the form of men being found,
> he humbled himself,
> becoming obedient even to death,
>   the death of a cross.
> Therefore God exalted him highly
> and gave him the name
>   which is above every name,
> That at the name of Jesus
>   every knee should bow,
>   in heaven and on the earth and under the earth,
> And every tongue confess
>   that Jesus Christ is Lord
>   to the glory of God the Father.[8]

At more or less the same time, from the same prison cell, and in similarly hymnic fashion, Paul extols Christ as "image of the invisible God, the firstborn of all creation . . . the beginning, the firstborn from the dead" (Col. 1:15, 18 NASB).[9] Hymnlike meter suggests itself in Colossians' companion piece, the epistle to the Ephesians:

> One Lord, one faith, one baptism,
> One God and Father of all,
> Who is above all and through all and in all.

> Ephesians 4:5–6

> Awake, O sleeper,
> And rise from the dead,
> And Christ will give you light.

> Ephesians 5:14

The songlike pattern of expression continues through the ministry period that follows this imprisonment. See, for instance, 1 Timothy 2:5–6; 3:16; and 6:15–16:

> For one is God,
> And one is the mediator between God and men,
> The man Christ Jesus,
> > Who gave himself as a ransom for all,
> > The testimony at the right time.

> Who was manifested in the flesh
> > Vindicated by the Spirit,
> > > Seen by angels,
> Proclaimed among the nations,
> > Believed on in the world,
> > > Taken up in glory.[10]

> He who is the blessed and only Sovereign,
> The King of kings
> And Lord of lords,
> He who alone has immortality,
> Dwelling in unapproachable light,
> Whom none among men has seen or can see,
> To him be honor and might forever. Amen.

This mode of expression carries right through to the second (also apparently Roman) imprisonment, one that Paul does not appear to have survived. Pointedly, he invites others to be his cosufferers and does so by hymning the power of the God

> Who saved us
>   and called us with a holy calling,
> Not according to our works,
>   but according to his own purpose and grace,
> Which he gave us in Christ Jesus
>   before times eternal,
>   but has now manifested
> Through the epiphany of our Savior Christ Jesus,
>   Who abolished death
>   and brought life and immortality to light
>   through the gospel.
>
> 2 Timothy 1:9–10

Preparing to die a martyr's death, Paul muses through Christ's promise to be present in the sufferings, Christ's warning not to ignore his presence at the Last Day, and the comfort of Christ's faithfulness in the midst of our daily failings:[11]

> If we die with him, we will also live with him;
> If we endure, we will also reign with him;
> If we will deny him, he will also deny us;
> If we are faithless, he remains faithful—
>   for he cannot deny himself.
>
> 2 Timothy 2:11–13

What we see in Paul's writings we see elsewhere as well. Those New Testament writers who are most tuned in to our wretchedness and poverty and to the fact that our lives in Christ will be shaped by suffering and persecution are, intriguingly, those who are most likely to break into a poetic or hymnic form. They do so because Jesus is alive—his resurrection-presence takes the sting out of their sufferings.

Luke's is the Gospel most taken with Jesus's compassion for the poor and for the wretched of the earth. Luke begins his two-volume work with Mary's gorgeous Magnificat, Zechariah's powerful paean of praise, the angels' heraldic carol, and Simeon's valedictory song of deliverance:

> For the Mighty One has done great things for me.
>
> Luke 1:49[12] NASB

> He has raised up a horn of salvation for us
> in the house of his servant David.
>
> Luke 1:69 NIV

> Glory to God in the highest,
>   and on earth peace to men on whom his favor rests.
>
> Luke 2:14 NIV

> For my eyes have seen your salvation,
>   which you have prepared in the sight of all people,
> a light for revelation to the Gentiles
>   and for glory to your people Israel.
>
> Luke 2:30–32 NIV

There is a dominating note of joy in Luke's writings that is due entirely to the fact that Jesus only *begins* his work in the Gospel but continues it throughout the book of Acts. "In my former book, Theophilus, I wrote about all that Jesus *began* to do and to teach," reads the opening line in the book of Acts (NIV). Now resurrected and exalted, Jesus continues his work by setting captives free through the spread of the gospel and the growth of the church.

Peter left us an epistle that calls on us to endure suffering as resident aliens and countercultural strangers. Its premise is that Jesus has been raised from the dead and is preserving an imperishable inheritance for us (1 Peter 1:3–4). In the midst of Peter's exhortations to endure suffering and ostracism, he launches into a hymn on Christ's suffering and glory:

> For Christ also suffered for sins once for all,
> the just for the unjust,
> that he might bring us to God,
> put to death in the flesh,
> but made alive in the spirit . . .[13]
> who is at the right hand of God,
> having gone into heaven,
> with angels and authorities and powers subject to him.
>
> 1 Peter 3:18, 22[14]

Exiled to the isle of Patmos, John is permitted to see visions of Christ's rule on behalf of his persecuted church. He hears hymns that anticipate the eventual triumph of the Lion who once was slain as a Lamb:

> And they sang a new song:
> "Worthy are you to take the book and to open its seals,
> for you were slain and you redeemed for God with your blood
>   people from every tribe and tongue and people and nation,
> and you made them a kingdom and priests to our God,
>   and they will reign on the earth."
>
> Revelation 5:9–10

Crowning it all is the writer to the Hebrews, the theologian of Jesus as the Singing Savior. As we have seen in previous chapters, this writer finds in David's thanks for a miraculous deliverance a forecast of the resurrected Christ's ministry of praise in heaven.

We have come to "the heavenly Jerusalem" where Jesus medi-
ates a new covenant (Heb. 12:22, 24). Now ascended, therefore,
and crowned with glory and honor, Jesus pronounces the name
of the Father to those whose enslavement to the fear of death is
over (Heb. 2:14–15). The Singing Savior stands in the true "great
assembly," one made up of all the children whose flesh and blood
he took on so he could render their enemy, the devil, powerless.
We, the church, are that great assembly. Whenever we gather and
lift our voices to the God of mercy, we become the place where
Jesus sings his tribute to the Father.

Having completed his work as atoning priest, Jesus inaugurates
his term as interceding priest. Leaving behind the earthly Jerusalem that expelled him into the hell of God-forsakenness and
having ascended to "the city of God, the heavenly Jerusalem," Jesus
now sings the Father's praises as Firstborn among the firstborn.
The song of the church below—"the fruit of lips that acknowledge his name" (Heb. 13:15 ESV)—is antiphon to this voice from
heaven.

Here in a nutshell is the entire glorious mystery of the New
Testament. By virtue of his resurrection, Jesus is alive in such a
way that he can be both "with us" and "for us." Simultaneously he
is "in the midst of the assembly" and in the heavenly Jerusalem
ever interceding for us. A permanent Singer has been installed.
From one perspective, he sings with us in the church; from another he intercedes for us in heaven. When the church gathers
in worship, earth and heaven converge. When we sing we are not
singing by ourselves. There is a higher song going on above ours
and a deeper song going on beneath ours.

Our Singing Is More Than Our Own

To my mind, Georges Rouault offered one of the twentieth
century's most satisfying theological statements when he juxta-

posed Plates 28 and 29 in his *Miserere* series. Plate 28 places us inside a burial crypt. Looking toward the back of the crypt, we see benches running along the left and right walls. The benches are covered with skulls. At the center of the image are two steps leading up to a small platform set into the back wall. The inset is shaped like a doorway rounded at the top. Inside the inset is a large black cross, and at the foot of the cross is yet another skull, a symbol of Golgotha, the place where death died in the death of Jesus. In his own hand, Rouault has inscribed beneath the picture: *Celui qui croit en moi, fût-il mort, vivra* ("He who believes in me, though he die, yet shall he live"—John 11:25).

Plate 29 takes us outside. Perhaps it is outside that crypt—we are not told. We see an empty landscape that simply opens out onto a distant horizon. Above, the sky is filled with a glowing, white sun. Distant, and just above the place where the sky meets the earth, is a single bird in flight. The picture is, of course, Rouault's depiction of Christ's resurrection and the newness it brings. Beneath, Rouault has inscribed: *Chantez Matines, le jour renait* ("Sing Matins, a new day is born"). "Matins" or "Morning Prayer" is a morning liturgy of song, a way of greeting each day as though it were that first Easter morning, filled with the promise of resurrection life. With these two pictures Rouault opens before us a vista of life filled with the song of the One who is "the resurrection" (John 11:25).

There are several implications of what we've said about the fact that Jesus is alive and that he continues his story in the church's worship.

First, because he lives, he is present in our worship. Our worship has a "sacramental cast" to it, to borrow a term from British writer Harry Blamires.[15] We don't meet on our own. We don't gather to remember "some dead guy" but to celebrate a living Presence. Nor do we have to conjure his presence, as though Jesus were some departed spirit or a fickle godling who's waiting for us to get the formula right. He is Lord of life and Master of all being; it so happens that it is his utter pleasure to gather his people and orchestrate their praise to the Father. That brings a transfigured perspective to our worship.

Somehow our singing is more his than ours. It is unspeakable joy for me to take my place as a worshiper among my brothers and sisters, knowing that Jesus, the Chief Liturgist, has already taken his place. My Sundays would be miserable if I thought otherwise. In his real presence, our posture is simultaneously more trembling and more relaxed. He is in *control* rather than we, so we can relax. *He*—who, like C. S. Lewis's Lion-Christ Aslan, is not safe, but is good—*he* is in control, so we tremble. We become at one and the same time more circumspect and less manipulative, more disciplined and yet more free.

Second, when we understand that Jesus rose from the dead as a Singer, we find that multiple aspects of his Person come into focus. We sing in his company because it helps us appreciate him for who he truly is. Even if our theology is otherwise as "orthodox" as it can be, if we do not see him as Singer and if accordingly we are not ourselves singers, we risk misperceiving him. (I'm not saying everybody has to be a great singer. I have a friend who sings every song on the same note, and loudly at that. But his countenance glows when he does so. He is fully present to Jesus in his singing, and he contributes a different kind of loveliness to our song.)

My point is this: a spirituality that is dependent on only one dimension of the whole Person risks truncating Jesus himself. That kind of spirituality leaves us with shriveled spirits, and it leaves the world with a dreadful misrepresentation of who it is we seek to represent. If we know Jesus only as Teacher, we succumb either to cold dogmatism or driven moralism. If we know Jesus only as Evangelist or Reformer, we reduce the church to a distribution center or a political party. We need the whole package—the whole

Person. In our struggle with sin and doubt, our Savior sings us his grace. When we are overcome with sorrow and with the ugliness of the world, our Savior brings to our ears "the clear though far-off song that hails a new creation." When the faith threatens to become bare propositions, the Savior turns it to poetry.

Third, because Jesus lives, we overcome. In a world that can overwhelm us with its pain, songs of Jesus's resurrection, exaltation, abiding presence, and promised return orient us to what is really true: we win. We respond to his singing because of the hope of resurrection and its power to renew us daily. That hope makes us more alive, more vibrantly real in the place Paul calls "the inner man." It is a stifling of that life *not* to sing.

We saw earlier that the chroniclers' account of David was written for a time that saw Israel's hopes fulfilled: exile was over; Israel was home again. Thankful praise was the order of the day. The New Testament too is written for such a time, and so its dominant note is also one of victory and thanksgiving. Indeed, its writers—all of them—are convinced that the most monumental thing in all human history took place in the resurrection of Jesus Christ. Jesus sings in our midst because death itself has begun working backwards. It is only fitting that we should answer his song with ours, because, as Twila Paris rightly sings, "All that has been taken, it shall be restored."[16]

7

THE SINGING SAVIOR'S
MANY VOICES

My mother is coming to campus. Would you mind cutting your hair?" Until I felt my gut clench at my college girlfriend's request, I didn't realize my Afro hairdo was more to me than a mere means of self-expression. In fact, my hair was a weapon of generational conflict. "Sure, your mom is important to me," is how I wish I had replied. To my regret, "No way; she's got to accept me for who I am," is what I actually did say.

A couple of years later a fellow seminarian and I shared, well, a mutual loathing. He carried himself with blue-blood affectations that made my skin crawl. He interned at one of the big, proper downtown churches that met at the God-appointed hour of 11:00 on Sunday mornings. I looked like a freak, went to a hip church on Sunday afternoons, and played tennis on Sunday mornings. To my surprise, he knocked on my door one night. "What could you possibly want?" was about all I could muster. But he had come to step across my barriers: "Would you be willing to pray with me? I've got this pastoral situation at church, and I need some help." He had looked past my hair, my views on Sabbath-keeping, and just about everything else. I was completely disarmed. Within minutes we were fast friends.

A few years later, I faced a second—and this time, unspoken—request about my hair. I was a year out of seminary. One day, I was talking with an older lady on the church staff. I noticed she wasn't making eye contact with me. Instead, her eyes kept scanning the outline of the Afro. I realized she was so distracted, she couldn't hear a word I said. I almost audibly heard God: "Your move." That very night I went to the mirror, scissors in hand.

Just like hair, music can either be a means of pushing each other away or of drawing closer to each other. "Music doesn't open doors nearly as much as it builds walls," maintains middle-aged *Orlando Sentinel* columnist and cartoonist Jake Vest, commenting on why musical performances during a recent Grammy awards telecast sent him to his refrigerator as much for escape as for refreshment.[1] What Vest's generation's rock musical *Hair* did to its parents, rap singer Andre 3000's version of the hootchie-kootchie does to Vest's generation: "shock, dismay, befuddle and offend."

But music doesn't have to work that way. Music—really diverse music—that the Savior inhabits can have the opposite effect. It is amazing to me what odd sorts of people Jesus loves and how oddly many of them sing. Yet he seems to be fond of all this strangeness. My theology and my experience tell me this: there is a special largeness of spirit and a particular conformity to Christ that come to those who step across their musical barriers to learn to hear the voice of their Singing Savior precisely in the oddity of somebody else's voice. A Christian friend once told me, "I can be pretty sure whether you'll like me, depending on how you feel about my music." Stepping across our own musical boundaries not only makes us friends to one another; it also shows our likeness to our Singing Savior.

We have come to the point at which it is finally possible to bring several lines into convergence. We have seen how singing sweetens our relationship with God and how the book of Psalms shapes our singing. We have seen how David's career embraced both an aloneness in the "not yet" of exile and the togetherness of the "already" of return from exile. We have seen how his lament of God-forsakenness led to a song of thanks in the midst of a great assembly. We have seen how Jesus sang himself into the exile of our curse so that he might rise as our champion. We have considered the way that our worship will be transfigured if we first of all reckon with the lead voice in our midst: his.

We want to see now the way Jesus's resurrection and ascension have enabled him to become the Architect of Praise, building by the Holy Spirit a house for God's dwelling. Further, it is time to reckon with the radical extent to which the "sacramental cast" of the Christian mind sees Christ in the people with whom Christ identifies.

Under Construction: A House of Praise

In the Israel Museum in Jerusalem hangs a stunning mosaic of King David playing a lyre, surrounded by wild animals that have been charmed by his music-making. The mosaic—taken from an early sixth-century synagogue floor in Gaza—likens David to the pagan hero Orpheus, who was supposed to have tamed beasts with his singing.[2] It reminds me of what the third-century Christian theologian Clement of Alexandria wrote about Jesus's superiority to that same Orpheus. Clement calls Jesus "God's New Song." To

my knowledge, Clement was the first theologian to notice that
the New Testament thinks of Jesus as a Singing Savior. Jesus is a
greater singer than Orpheus, maintains Clement, because Jesus
tames wilder beasts:

> He is the only one who ever tamed the most intractable of all wild
> beasts—human beings. For he tamed birds, that is, people who
> are flighty; reptiles, that is, those who are crafty; lions, that is, the
> passionate; swine, that is, those who are pleasure-loving; wolves,
> that is, the rapacious. . . . All these most savage beasts, . . . the
> heavenly song of itself transformed into gentle people. . . .
>
> See how mighty is the new song! It has made . . . humans
> out of wild beasts. They who were otherwise dead, who had
> no share in the real and true life, revived when they heard the
> song.[3]

The power of Jesus's song, though, is manifest not only in
its ability to raise the dead to life. Jesus is able to forge all those
"flighty," "crafty," "passionate," "pleasure-loving," and "rapacious"
individuals into a single orchestra of praise. Clement imagines
Jesus singing to those whom he has redeemed:

> "You are my harp and my flute and my temple—my harp by reason
> of the music, my flute by reason of the breath of the Spirit, my
> temple by reason of the Word"—God's purpose being that the
> music should resound, the Spirit inspire, and the temple receive
> its Lord.[4]

The synagogue mosaic of the singing David hints at the remarkable task that the risen Son of David undertakes as our Singing Savior: building a temple of praise made up of "the most
intractable of all wild beasts—human beings." Jesus did not rise
merely to make individuals alive again. He rose to forge them
into a building that sings.

David wanted to build a temple for God. David gave to Solomon the tools he would need in the next generation to build the temple—the contract with Hiram of Tyre, the financial and material resources, and above all, songs to fill the house and make it a place for God to meet with his people.

Even more did Jesus desire to build a temple to put on display God's power to redeem and reconcile. That's why he told Peter: "I will build my church . . . and the gates of hell will not stand against it" (Matt. 16:18). Jesus now builds the true temple that David could only imagine. While David had to leave it to his heir to do the building, Jesus's resurrection makes him a living presence in the project—he builds *with* his co-heirs. Jesus rises as architect and chief builder of a house of praise. Our Singing Savior stands in the midst of the structure and orchestrates its praise to the Father.

Using various figures of speech, New Testament writers sketch the construction that has been in progress ever since Jesus's resurrection. John tells us how Jesus's cleansing of Jerusalem's temple forecast the tearing down of a house of mere stone to make way for one made up of Jesus's "body" (John 2:21). Peter likens us to "living stones being built into a spiritual house, a holy priesthood" (1 Peter 2:5), Jesus Christ himself being the cornerstone or capstone of the building (1 Peter 2:6–7). In his ministry, Paul believed he saw that edifice under construction, and he said: Jew and Gentile are being built into a dwelling place for God where they showcase "the manifold wisdom of God" even "to the principalities and powers in the heavenly places" (Eph. 3:10 NKJV).[5]

The writer to the Hebrews too takes up the image. While "Moses was faithful *in* God's house," he says, "Christ is faithful *over* God's house as a Son. And we are his house, if we hold on to our confidence and the hope of which we boast" (Heb. 3:6). What has prompted the writing of this tract in the first place is the fact that some of its readers are being tempted to stop meeting together

(Heb. 10:25). The writer points to Jesus singing in the assembly
(Heb. 2:12) because he wants to head off an attrition of the assembly that would diminish the Savior's song. He wants his readers to continue stimulating one another to love and good works (Heb. 1:24). He wants the house in which Jesus sings to stay intact.

It is likely, I think, that the looming Jewish War (AD 66–70) has put pressure on Jewish Christians all around the Mediterranean basin to rally to the cause of ethnic nationalism.[6] An exceptionally literate and especially heritage-respecting cadre of Jewish Christian believers is considering whether it should close ranks with its kin or cast its lot with fellow Christians. Part of what the writer hopes to do is recapture his readers' imaginations with the grandeur of that new people to which they now belong in Christ. This citizenship is the goal to which biblical history had always been driving. In Christ they have come to "Mt. Zion and to the city of the living God, the heavenly Jerusalem, . . . and to the general assembly" (Heb. 12:22). Neither alone nor in elite cadres, but together, the writer insists, we pursue the city with foundations, even though it puts us "outside the camp" of any traditional loyalty, whether Jewish or otherwise (Heb. 13:13).

It would have been a difficult choice for those early Jewish believers. They were being called to ostracism. They were being called to do in their day what Moses had done in his: choose to "endure ill-treatment with the people of God [rather] than to enjoy the passing pleasures of sin" (Heb. 11:25 NASB). As had been the case with Moses, the pleasures they were being asked to forego were those of privilege, position, and prestige. As with Moses, their level of literacy and social power meant that it was no small thing to consider "the reproach of Christ greater riches than the treasures of Egypt" (Heb. 11:26 NASB). To seek the greater reward, they had to say no to a reward that was not obviously lesser on first examination. Their solidarity with the rest of the people of God most likely meant associating with people who were otherwise less literate and less vested. It certainly meant associating themselves with people who were not "in" in their social circles.

So it is that Jesus sings to the Father in the place where estranged hearts are gathered, and where heaven and earth meet: "in the assembly."

Jesus Sings in the "Great Assembly" (Psalm 22:25)

As we have seen, Psalm 22 is a study in profound contrasts. It moves from crucifixion to resurrection and from lament to victory chant. I have known of this pattern within the psalm for many years. What I did not see for a long time was how the psalm moves from the Singer's aloneness to his being surrounded by so many people, and people of so many kinds at that. It is within the "great assembly" (v. 25) that the former Sufferer sings his hymn to the God who answers his cry for help. Having been once left alone in his agony with a band of evildoers closing in, now the Singer is surrounded in worship by Jew and Gentile (vv. 23, 27), poor and rich (vv. 26, 29), and generations past and generations to come (vv. 29–31). In place of God's abandonment is God's renewed gaze and listening ear (v. 24), and in place of the scoffers and torturers is a vast and variegated assembly of worship. The psalm begins as a solo, but it ends as a chorale.

Isn't it remarkable that this is the answer to Messiah's loneliness on the cross? The promise of the Singing Savior's reveling in the company of a naturally disparate but now gathered people is a large part of the joy set before him and which enabled him to endure the shame of the cross (Heb. 12:2).

The presence of so many different kinds of worshipers in the Singing Savior's great assembly cannot help but raise pressing questions about what—or better, whose—aesthetic governs their worship.

When the descendants of Jacob/Israel join the Savior's song and glorify God and express their awe of him (v. 23), what musical language do they use? When "all the ends of the earth" and "all the families of the earth" hear in the Savior's song a remembrance of the image they were made to bear (v. 27), and thus turn to the Lord, with what musical tongue do they worship? When "the afflicted" who seek the Lord eat alongside "the fat ones" at the Lord's table (vv. 26, 29), with whose tongue do they offer their common praise and worship? And when those who have already gone to the dust bow before the One whose death has secured their resurrection (v. 29), do they sing the same song in the same way as the people who are yet to be born but who themselves nonetheless will hear of the accomplishment of the same righteousness for them (vv. 30–31)?

Let me suggest that every group brings its own voice, but no group brings the official voice. One Voice sings above them all, and this Voice sings in all their voices, excluding none. Because there are so many dimensions to his own being, the multiplicity of voices amplifies his song.

Jesus sings the Hebrew songs of covenant faithfulness, giving "the Israel of God" the right, at long last, to name the name latent in the old covenant's psalms of anticipation. It is his resurrection and ascension that their homecomings had forecast. As we saw in an earlier chapter, the theme "from shame to glory" is not just the story of Psalm 22. It is the story of the Psalter itself, moving as it does from Book One's plaintive songs of David in the wilderness (Psalms 1–41) to Book Five's songs celebrating in advance an ultimate and final Davidic rule, that of Messiah (Psalms 107–150). "From shame to glory" is Israel's and Judah's career because it is Jesus's career.

That is why on a number of occasions New Testament writers can summarize the whole of the Old Testament story as a foreshadowing of the sufferings and resurrection of Messiah

(Luke 24:27, 44–47; Acts 26:22–23; 1 Peter 1:10–12). Thus, in the church, Jesus sings the sweet song of salvation, the song of God's faithfulness to his promises to bring his people home by way of his own suffering for them.

In the same row of the choir, the Singing Savior places people who before knowing him have sung only dirty or idolatrous ditties. Jesus purges the idolatrous aspects of a culture's music and focuses the yearning for redemption that shows up wherever the *imago Dei* bears the kiss of common grace. Jesus cleanses consciences and he cleanses songs one would have thought foul beyond redemption. The "entertaining and slightly ribald" tune ELLACOMBE wound up in Catholic songbooks of the late eighteenth century, then was touched up by Protestants, and has been used with various texts, such as "I Sing the Mighty Power of God" and "The Day of Resurrection."[7] It's hard to miss the fact that Jesus sings with a staggering plurality of "folk voices"—songs emerging from cultures and social subsystems configured around "all the families of the earth." As the song says, "red and yellow, black and white, they are precious in his sight." Because of that fact, they all have a voice in his assembly.

What I believe we have seen in twenty centuries of church music is Christ calling forth his song from every culture his gospel has touched. Even when believers attempt distinctly "Christian" music, their music bears the marks of their social world, and indeed would be incomprehensible without those marks. Queen Elizabeth I could mock "Geneva jigs" precisely because many of the psalm settings emanating from Calvin's church sounded like the dance songs for which Continental European troubadours were famous.[8] Jesus sings God's covenantal faithfulness and the width of his mercy in as many musical dialects as there are peoples who embrace him.

Both the poor and the rich are invited to the Rescued Singer's table of thanksgiving. We saw how the Greek Old Testament

placed the working poor there. Throughout history, the working poor have produced a simple, gritty, unpretentious aesthetic.
"Work songs" comprise a subset of folk music—genres like sea
chanteys, chain gang songs, and cowboy ballads. But the music of
the working poor takes into its sweep all kinds of earthy musical
dialects: from blues to folk hymns. The music of the "working
poor" tends to be participatory. Its beauty lies more in being done
than in being listened to. Folk music tends to be gritty, because it
deals with life's injustices, hopes, and compensating pleasures.

The highly educated and cultured—the ones the psalmist calls
"the fat ones"—are at the table of the Singing Savior, too. Just as
a certain aesthetic tends to circulate among a society's working
poor, a different kind of artistic sense seems to emanate from any
culture's literati, those who have the leisure to get their aesthetic
training in schools rather than on the streets. In fact, the word
school comes from the ancient Greek word *scholē*, which meant
"leisure," and was extended to include what "leisured" people
could do: study.

From the cross, the ultimate Singer of Psalm 22 anticipates
singing both among those whose sense of beauty is homegrown
and among those who can afford to go off to school to acquire a
refined aesthetic. Luke, the New Testament writer who pays so
much attention to the poor, also shows how Jesus drew his followers from the upper crust—for example, Zaccheus ("he was
a chief tax collector and he was rich," Luke 19:1 NASB), Joanna
(wife of Herod's steward, Luke 8:3), Barnabas (early benefactor of
the church in Jerusalem, Acts 4:36–37), and Lydia (merchant of
purple fabric, and hostess to Paul in Philippi, Acts 16:14–15).

Finally, Jesus sings both among the saints who have gone before and also among the saints who are yet-to-be-born. His is
"the assembly of the first-born who are enrolled in heaven . . .
and the spirits of just men made perfect" (Heb. 12:23). His community is not limited by death, and neither is his song. The book

of Revelation tells us that heaven's current worship is character-ized by the same dynamic we know on earth. On the one hand, the martyrs cry out "How long, O Lord?" (Rev. 6:10), and on the other, they already (in my understanding) participate in "the first resurrection" and rule and serve as priests alongside Christ during the present era of gospel victory (Rev. 20:4–6). Some lit-urgies preserve the ancient prayer, "And so we join our voices with choirs of angels, with prophets, apostles, martyrs, and with the faithful of every time and place who forever sing to the glory of your name: Holy, holy, holy, God of power and might. . . ." This expression of the living connection between the church in heaven and the church on earth is correct. As G. K. Chesterton observes, honoring tradition is how we give the dead their voice in our community. And that is important, because their voice is a part of Jesus's voice.

Jesus also assembles those who will receive the Word them-selves, make it their own, give it their own voice, and then faith-fully pass it to the generation following in their wake. In the sec-ond century, an anonymous Roman Christian commended Jesus to a pagan friend named Diognetus. He told Diognetus that Jesus was "from of old," but because he is alive now and is born in our hearts, he is also "forever young" (*Epistle to Diognetus* 11:4).

Imagine the consternation of the first listeners to Jesus's teach-ing on the separation of the sheep from the goats (Matt. 25:31–46). How many must have scratched their heads when they heard Jesus say that serving or not serving his brothers and sisters was serving or not serving him—so much so that serving him in them shows one's fitness for heaven and not serving him in them shows one's fitness for hell. Because the King matters to me, his people have to matter to me. Accordingly, it has to matter to me that my Singing Savior surrounds himself with so many whose ways of singing are utterly different from mine. It has to matter to me that Jesus

hears harmonies that sound cacophonous to me. It has to matter
to me that he dances to rhythms that do not move me.

Bach, Bubba, and the Blues Brothers

I've developed my own shorthand for the range of the Singing
Savior's voice. I think of Jesus singing with a "Bach" voice, with a
"Bubba" voice, and with a "Blues Brothers" voice. Bach's is Jesus's
voice in the City of God—here Jesus sings with the refinement
and sophistication of classical culture. Bubba's is his voice in the
Family of God—here Jesus sings with the grittiness and simplicity
of folk culture. And the Blues Brothers' is his voice among the
Friends of God—here Jesus sings with the contemporaneity and
outward-boundness of popular culture. Let me explain.[9]

In my thinking, "Bach's" is the voice of culture and refinement, an aesthetic submitted to the standards of urbanity and
schooled discipline. Jesus sings among the likes of those to whom
the epistle to the Hebrews is addressed: those who know the
privileges of heritage, status, and education. Both from artists
who know Jesus personally and from those who hold him at
arm's length, the Singing Savior draws music that reflects his
own grandeur and royalty and urbanity. Composers and musicians from Israel's heritage (say, Felix Mendelssohn or Leonard
Bernstein) and from outside, from "all the families of the earth"
(say, Johann Sebastian Bach and Ralph Vaughan Williams), have
had their artistic gifts more than challenged to give adequate
expression to Christ's loftiness and majesty. "Bach's" voice gives
expression to the New Testament's vision of our being called to
participate in the City of God. Here is a commonwealth in which
the worthiest of human aspirations—including the artistic—find
their goal and satisfaction.

"Bubba" is my shorthand for the fact that Jesus also sings
among the culturally less refined—he is as much Brother within

the family sitting around the piano singing "Will the Circle Be Unbroken" as he is Lord of the cathedral congregation chanting a *Te Deum*. While Johann Sebastian Bach is a well-known historical figure, "Bubba" is an indistinct figure of speech. "Bubba" represents to me the most famous of folk composers: "Anonymous." Psalm 22 envisions the Singing Savior having at his table both rich and poor, and I suggest this means he is pleased to take up with both the artistically elegant and the artistically inelegant. Jesus's life bespeaks a valuing of grit and earthiness, even if his preexistence, his royal lineage, and his present rule bespeak his grace and loftiness. So I figure he must love Delta blues and "old timey music" as well as the cantata and the oratorio. Bubba's voice gives expression to the New Testament's vision of our being called to participate in the family of God—a sense of belonging to one another sheerly because we have been chosen for one another; not because we're pretty or smart or hip but because Jesus has made us family.

"The Blues Brothers" are in my choir also because, well, I fancy their story. Remember the movie? Jake and Elwood Blues (John Belushi and Dan Ackroyd) are two white deadbeats who, upon Jake's release from prison for theft, learn that the church-based orphanage in which they had been raised is about to go bankrupt. About the only legal thing they know how to do is play African-American soul music. Jake and Elwood go on a "mission from God" to reunite their soul band for a concert in order to raise money to save the orphanage, and so to take care of the next generation. In the process, of course, they break a lot of rules. To me, they are a parable of a similar call God places on each generation of the church. The Blues Brothers' voice answers to the New Testament's call to be cadres of friends (the NT term for this is *koinōnia*) who enlist the common dialect of their culture (its *koinē*) to the service of redemptive ends. Musically, we are called to do the best we can with the musical idioms we have inherited so we can help the next generation hear the Savior's song and take up their own voice in response.

There are many ways to tell the story of how Christ carries on his song in the church. He enlists all kinds of people in his choir, and they're not all like me. I hope that others will add their experiences and histories to mine. As it is, though, I'm rooted in the Euro-American classical heritage. I've had my soul shaped by American evangelical hymnody and American folk music. I've led worship in churches where the basic musical language of people is that of post-Elvis popular culture. So I'll tell the part of the story that I know—the story of Bach, Bubba, and the Blues Brothers.

8

BACH'S VOICE

"Sermons in Music"

I t should not surprise us that the glory of Christ inspires people from all walks of life to throw all that they are, or have, into his worship. And when it comes to the wealthy, the privileged, the educated, and the powerful, we can expect that once Christ's message finds its way into their hearts, they sponsor or create music that honors his name but that also bears the stamp of their resources.[1] This is no more unnatural than people praying in their native tongue.

Out of their training and resources, "classical" or "high art" musicians create music that answers to important dimensions of Christ's own person.[2] He is, after all, the preexistent One whose majesty prior to his coming to us is inconceivable. Even though his enfleshment begins at the planting of the seed in Mary's womb, his existence has no beginning. Hundreds of years before his

birth, Psalm 45:6 says of him, "Your throne, O God, is forever
and ever"[3] (NASB). We can understand why the hymn writer envisions the Savior having come from the "ivory palaces" of that
same psalm (Ps. 45:8). Before his advent the Son of God held a
"glory" he himself demurred at describing, acknowledging only
that he was returning to it: "And now, Father, glorify me in your
presence with the glory I had with you before the world began"
(John 17:5 NIV).

Even in human terms, he is royalty: "Remember Jesus Christ. . .
descended from David" (2 Tim. 2:8 NIV; see also Matt. 1:6; Luke
3:31; Rom. 1:3). In fact, the likelihood is that the Nazareth of his
upbringing was a colony of displaced offspring of David who saw
themselves as sojourners holding to the true faith, expecting that
one day from among them the promised Seed of David would
emerge.[4] The New Testament depicts Jesus as King David's final
heir, ruling now "far above all rule and authority and power and
dominion" (Eph. 1:21 ESV). Jesus *is* what the most exalted dreams
of glory and honor and power and royalty are merely *about*.

Because he is the very Logos of God and agent of creation, Jesus
is deserving of the most elegant, the most intellectually rigorous
and challenging—and the most passionately romantic—aesthetic
expressions of worship imaginable. Christ merits majestic worship. For many people, and for good reason, the attraction of a
classical aesthetic is that it connotes transcendence, elegance,
and excellence—and is therefore especially apposite to worship
of the exalted Christ.

"Sermons in Music"

No one has crafted music that adorns the nobility of our Savior more ably than Johann Sebastian Bach (1685–1750). It has
been said, and rightly so, that Western music is pre-Bach and
post-Bach. His nearly three hundred church cantatas, of which

two hundred survive, define what it is to wed the biblical story to musical craftsmanship—the cantatas are, to borrow a term from author Daniel Boorstin, "sermons in music."[5] Singer and writer Jane Stuart Smith likens them to Rembrandt paintings:

> The cantatas join the Bible, music, and history into a unified whole—the same thing Rembrandt did in his etchings and paintings, expressing scriptural truth by means of great art.[6]

Bach brought to their apogee two musical genres that are largely the province of the church: the cantata and the passion. His *Passion According to St. Matthew* and *Passion According to St. John* are masterpieces of pastoral musicianship, as they weave together challenging music with contemporary congregational hymns. At the same time, his contributions to Western music as such are inestimable. Though, for instance, he was in many respects a conservative craftsman, Bach's *Well Tempered Clavier*, keyboard compositions in all twenty-four keys, contributed to one of the most revolutionary innovations in the history of world music: the establishment of the system of equal temperament.[7]

His reach has been extraordinary. A twenty-year-old Felix Mendelssohn helped "rediscover" Bach decades after his death. Mendelssohn's performance of Bach's matchless *Passion According to St. Matthew* in 1829 on the hundredth anniversary of its original performance marked a watershed in Western musical history. Bach was reborn for a new day, and Mendelssohn's life took a turn as well. The force and fervor of Bach's setting of the Gospel affected Mendelssohn in a profound way.[8] He set his hand (at his father's urging) to write his first oratorio, the *St. Paul*, with its succession of chorales, arias, and recitatives, an homage to Bach.[9]

Over a hundred years later, laboring under Communist rule in the 1960s in Estonia, Christian composer Arvo Pärt began a subtle revolt against the banality of Soviet realism. For ammunition to deconstruct the propagandistic nature of what passed for art under Communism, he turned to Western twelve-note serialism.[10] When it was time to move beyond revolt to reconstruction, Pärt found himself turning to Bach. In his pivotal *Credo*, Pärt builds a tonal center out of chaos by using Bach's "C Major Prelude" from the *Well Tempered Clavier*.[11] The *Credo* is "a hymn not only to the splendour of Bach's music, but also to the splendour of tonality, and finally to the splendour of religious belief," concludes musicologist and conductor Paul Hillier.[12] Bach pointed the way forward for Pärt, ironically through the route of early music. Pärt then discovered a music even earlier than Bach's in the chimes and texts of the Russian Orthodox Church. His distinctive style, which he calls "tintinabulli," is a mystical and profound interpenetration of Bach, the ethos of Russian Orthodox liturgy, and a post-atonal tonality.

Now, Jesus loves Bach's music and that of his aesthetic kin—of this I am certain. I am equally sure, however, that he finds their most elevated and demanding stuff to be but nursery tunes.

For me, the attraction of the classical aesthetic is in the way the "high art" heritage helps the church to be aesthetically self-aware and self-critical. The relationship between the "true" and the "beautiful" has long been under discussion.[13] The "linkage" may be subtle, but it is there. From Bach to Pärt, Christian composers with the training and gifts for exploring the "beautiful" have lent Christ's voice to the larger conversation in our culture about what is beautiful, and ultimately about what is true.

The Jubal Factor

This "larger conversation" is an old one. From nearly the beginning of time, according to the biblical view, believers and nonbelievers have conversed awkwardly across a cultural divide.

God gave believers the song of redemption, but, curiously, he gave unbelievers the gift of song. In the Bible, the story line of redemption is carried through the line of Adam and Eve's third child, Seth; but musical craftsmanship emerges first among the children of Cain, murderer of Abel and the first builder of cities (Gen. 4:17). Jubal, representing the unbelieving line of his father Cain, is father of "all those who play the lyre and pipe" (Gen. 4:21 NASB).[14] Concludes theologian William Edgar: "Cain's descendants invent culture, while Seth's invent worship."[15]

God has placed us in a symbiotic relationship with nonbelieving musicians. I call this the Jubal factor. They have a bravery we need while we have a story they are lost without. I suspect that God himself prompts the children of Jubal, the mad geniuses outside the believing community—the Beethovens, the Wagners—to push the musical frontiers further out so the church can follow and learn new textures, tone colors, rhythms, harmonic combinations, and melodic possibilities.

We need the children of Jubal. Unfortunately, Christians play it safe. And this reality stands in some tension with the way biblical faith ought to work. The apostle Paul teaches us that because we know the answer to the human condition, we are able to acknowledge just how troublesome that condition is. He admits to the Corinthian church, for instance: "My conscience is clear, but that does not make me innocent" (1 Cor. 4:4 NIV). This sort of candor comes, New Testament theologian Gerd Theissen argues, to a person who knows that what should trouble his or her conscience has been taken care of in Christ's work on the cross.[16] Because we know we are forgiven, we can be candid, vulnerable, and reflective. Sometimes, though, it doesn't seem to work the way it should. We think we need to deny our fallenness. We fear the shame of failing to be perfect. When that happens, we live on the surface of life, cutting ourselves off from true sorrow or true joy. Alternatively, we often keep ourselves busy with "spiritual" busyness to protect

ourselves from being overwhelmed by the wretchedness we think
we shouldn't experience any longer. Here's where the children of
Jubal come to our aid. Unbelievers, unhindered by our fear of
admitting there's a gap between the "is" and the "ought," probe
depths we sometimes pretend are not there.

Because we know the answer, it's easy for us to forget the questions. We can be so busy trying to muzzle the beast within through
a regimen of Bible reading, prayer, and "Just say no!"-ism when
along comes a Wagner or a Mahler who touches something deep
within us. Sometimes it takes a son or daughter of Jubal to open
up longings we have tried to forget—longings for a life that is
more than merely safe, for a life filled with ecstasy and mystery,
fraught with danger and passion. We are troubled when the passions open up to us, because we have not learned what Harry
Blamires taught: that there is a "sacramental cast" to our longings.
They are pointers to God himself. Or as C. S. Lewis says (paraphrasing): "Our problem is not that we want too much, but that
we are satisfied with too little."[17] Sometimes the wanting is done
better by those outside the faith, because they haven't forgotten
what it is to be hungry.

Of course, we could mention the Jubal factor under any cat-
egory of music. Christians stand in a necessary and precarious
relationship with artists in folk and popular music as well. But
I'm discussing it within the realm of classical music because the
philosophical issues that music raises are so easy to see here.

Composer Richard Wagner, for instance, wrote at length about
the relationship between "music," which he thought of as passionate and receptive, and "text," which he thought of as rational and
aggressive. Philosopher and in many respects father of postmodern-
ism, Friedrich Nietzsche wrote about how the history of Western
music is characterized by a contest between a formal and rational
impulse and a romantic and evocative impulse. The one he called
Apollonian after lyre-playing Apollos, the Greek god of reason and

war. The other he called Dionysian, after flute-playing Dionysus, the Greek god of passion and wine. Wagner's and Nietzsche's discussions are by no means the final say. But they do give us vocabulary for exploring why Christians wrestle with music. Milan's bishop Ambrose (AD 339–397) championed lush music in worship. His disciple Augustine was afraid the beauty of the music would distract him from the texts. Ever since, we have recognized we have a volatile mix on our hands.

We know that God brings together truth and beauty, but we're not beyond getting confused about how he does so. Sometimes the children of Jubal distill the issues for us.

Back to Bach

Then again, without our story the children of Jubal are lost. The son of a Lutheran pastor, Nietzsche had been raised to love Jesus, but in his teen years he declared he could no longer take communion. He needed, says Nietzsche scholar Alistair Kee, "a nobler god" than Christianity offered.[18] As a young adult Nietzsche became an avid fan of Wagner's operas. He thought Wagner's grandiose musical stories championing the gods of pre-Christian Europe pointed the way to a gloriously repaganized Europe. Nietzsche looked to Wagner to save the West from the ignobility of the Christian faith. He hoped Wagner would help create a post-Christian era with a new, nobler art. But Wagner's final opera, *Parsifal*, a story about the Holy Grail, shattered Nietzsche's hopes. With *Parsifal*, Wagner landed back in a Christianity he had tried to escape his entire life. Nietzsche recoiled at the profane thought of Wagner "prostrating himself before the cross"—and Nietzsche himself began a descent into dementia.

Theologian Jaroslav Pelikan argues that Nietzsche's life floundered—indeed, it shipwrecked—because he sought the holy in the beautiful. By contrast, contends Pelikan, Bach's life and music touched glory because he sought the beautiful in the holy. Nietzsche made a god of the beautiful and it broke him. Bach submitted to God and was given beauty as a gift.[19]

Chief among the reasons Bach embodies for me the voice of Christ as the One who sings in the City of God is that his body of work is a rich testament to the power of Christ to wed head and heart. Bach's greatness does not come from his somehow embodying an elegant, refined music that soars above the fleshly and passionate. The glory of Bach lies in the way he places disciplined musical craftsmanship in service of God's great romance. Nietzsche can't get past the war between Apollos and Dionysus. Bach plays out the dance between the Ambrosian (the more emotionally charged) and the Augustinian (the more intellectually rigorous) aspects of Christian faith. His music incarnates impeccable orthodoxy and indescribable passion.

Bach's theology was entirely submitted to Scripture and the creeds.[20] At the same time, he had drunk from the tap of those who were calling for a greater personal reality, greater attention to the existential implications of the faith.[21] It was conductor John Hodges who helped me see this. In a seminary class one day, he pulled out Giovanni Palestrina's and Bach's settings of parallel texts from respective Masses and exclaimed, "Can't you just see the restraint in Palestrina, and the passion in Bach?" I did see it—Bach used more notes. But I could *hear* the difference better. There is a density, a thickness to Bach that had not been there in his predecessors; Bach was aiming directly at his listeners' hearts, because he was pouring out his own heart in his compositions.

I think Christ is fond of classical music and wants his people to explore it for two reasons. First, this kind of artistic expression is true to his majesty; it embodies his grandeur. At every turn, classical music presents us with another Christian masterpiece to be reckoned with—from just about anything by Bach to just about anything by Pärt; and from Handel's *Messiah* to Paul Hindemith's

Mathis der Maler[22] and his *Noblissima Visione.*[23] Since the emergence of the faith, Christianity has not always set the agenda for
Western classical music—but it has pretty much served as its
conscience.

Second, classical music puts us on the stage where the great
conversation about the relationship between the "true" and the
"beautiful" is carried out. Especially when we give ourselves to a
critically appreciative listening to unbelievers' works we attune
ourselves to some of our culture's most honest expressions of its
aspirations and its lostness. By contrast, in believers' works we
overhear some of Christ's most urgent wooings of the humanity
for which he has given his life.

Music That Makes Us Bigger Than Ourselves

I'd like to offer a third reason Christ sings through Bach and
kin: there is an expansiveness of spirit Christ would inculcate in
us and which art of this kind fosters.

My mother's father was a Mississippi sharecropper. My father's
father was a Tennessee small farmer. My own musical heritage
is rather modest. Before going to college, if I had been asked to
pull the name of a piece of religious classical music out of the air,
I probably would have said: "The Lord's Prayer," by Albert Hay
Malotte, which I had heard at church and which is really semi-
classical, at best. As I recounted earlier, Mort Whitman took me
to hear Handel's *Messiah* shortly after my conversion in college.
After that I started exploring this new musical world on my own.
One of my first purchases was a boxed set of "Musical Masterpieces" I happened upon in the school bookstore. For hours, I
listened to them on my dorm room stereo. What happened for
me musically was what college did for me generally: horizons
were pushed out, and my heart was opened to the wideness of
life under God.

Bach's *Suite Number 2 for Orchestra* and Handel's *Water Music Suite* became precious statements to me of how the Savior of souls could restore beauty and playfulness to all of life. Tchaikovsky's *Violin Concerto in D Major, Opus 35* sang poignantly to me of the human longing to know nobility and of the great either/or before us all: accept it as a gift in Christ or struggle against irrevocable fate to try to know it on one's own. Gershwin's *Rhapsody in Blue* made me wonder at the textures and tones and colors he heard in urban life. My college textbooks (I was a sociology major) were bemoaning the way urbanization was trivializing and dehumanizing us. The gospel was telling me something different: that worth is what I bring to where I live because I belong to Christ. And the beauty Gershwin was able to extract from the modern city reminded me that the gospel was right. In my listening I began to appreciate how the Lord of all of life had come to save life in all its dimensions. It was an appreciation books alone could never provide.

Christ imparts himself to us; as we take him in we come more and more to bear what Paul calls the eternal weight of glory (2 Cor. 4:17). As Christ more fully inhabits us, he makes us larger, more "ourselves." I found the master composers contributing something to me that felt like that "greatness of soul," which Aristotle called "a jewel of the virtues" and which Aquinas says is part of what Christ imparts when he imparts himself.[24] As life has progressed, I have found music that is bigger than I am helping to keep me from shrinking back from the challenges before me. I know Mahler is not for everybody. But his symphonies undo me.[25] My desperately sick soul needs strong medicine. It takes music with his range and power to open the inner places where my fears about death and dying are hid. Mahler lost a four-year-old daughter to disease and composed his later symphonies under the cloud of heart disease. Perhaps that is why his ruminations on death ring so true to me.[26]

We live in a world that makes it hard to maintain sexual purity. When actor/comedian Jerry Seinfeld said his long-running sitcom was a show about "nothing," he wasn't being altogether honest. The show was at least about this: when it comes to sex, there are no rules—only taboos to be challenged. In an odd way perhaps, Richard Wagner has helped me keep my bearings in spite of my being surrounded by an ocean of moral relativity. His opera about the doomed adulterous couple, *Tristan and Isolde*, overwhelms me with the sad rootlessness of the modern world. This opera's deliberately disoriented atonality makes me aware of the allure of the transmoral, the temptation to make my own way, to play by my own rules. Counterpoint to *Tristan and Isolde*'s amoral chromaticism is the return to tonality in the main theme from *Parsifal*, Wagner's final work, the opera that Nietzsche found so repugnant, because in it, Wagner gropes his way to some sort of faith in Christ. That groping is easily recognizable in the musical motif that most characterizes this opera, the so-called "Dresden Amen," an incomplete tonal scale. What disgusted Nietzsche has sometimes helped me hold on to what I know to be true and beautiful.

Concluding Reflections on Bach's Voice

Some of us are in churches where classical music is the medium of choice. We've grown up in homes that have passed on to us an appreciation for Bach's voice. Or perhaps we've acquired a taste after we've gone off to school. To others, I realize, I'm speaking a foreign language. It's okay. God does not gift his children in uniform fashion. Christ doesn't form churches in cookie-cutter fashion, either.

However, for those of us who want to explore the world of Bach and his kin, abundant resources are at hand. National Public Radio is everywhere. Ken Myers's *Mars Hill Audio Journal*

frequently features classical composers.[27] Everybody has at least
one friend who is a classical music buff—a friend of mine owns
three thousand CDs and is ready at the drop of a hat to recom-
mend his favorite recordings, conductors, and labels. The most
middling of cities has a community orchestra and community
chorus—and where there is an orchestra or a chorus, there are
people who love to talk about the music they love. Most of us
are within striking distance of a college or university that offers
music appreciation courses. Of the writing of books, as Solomon
quipped, there is no end; one of my favorites on classical music
is *The Gift of Music: Great Composers and Their Influence* by
Jane Stuart Smith and Betty Carlson, both of L'Abri Fellowship.[28]
In addition, the Internet puts at our fingertips an unimaginable
wealth of information.

Maybe the perfect musical diet is equal parts Bach, Bubba, and
the Blues Brothers. I don't know. I've never seen it in church. I've
been musically "in charge," or partially so, in enough situations
that if it were possible to establish a perfect symmetry among
classical, folk, and pop, it would have happened. I've concluded
that it must be our Singing Savior's delight to make one fellowship
resonate more to Bach's voice and another to Bubba's. It must bring
him satisfaction to grace one fellowship with a heap of the Blues
Brothers' gifts and a dash of Bubba, and another with a boatload
of Bubba and a sprinkling of Bach.

For whatever reason, my adult years have found me in churches
that don't fancy "Bach's voice" as much as I do. No problem. Life
in community outweighs the pursuit of aesthetic equilibrium. At
the same time, I ache for the body of Christ to be touched more
with the glories of Mozart and Haydn, and Benjamin Britten and
John Rutter. The gap between my "Bach voice" longings and my
ability to fulfill them has made me cheer on the fellowships that do
Bach better. The gap has made me pray with thanksgiving for the
distinctive voice they give to Christ's song in my world. Knowing

my own heart, I also find myself praying they will cherish the precious gift they have and not tarnish it by loving the gift more than the Giver or by despising fellowships God has gifted differently.

Some of the noblest artists I know rein in their preferences and training to serve worship communities with humbler aesthetics than their own. I remember sitting in a Chapel Hill restaurant with fellow church musicians. They were regaling each other with anecdotes about their favorite opera composers. I was made suddenly aware of how far beneath them was the folkish music we had just done together in church that day. Not knowing my Verdi from my Wagner at the time, all I could do was sit quietly and give thanks for their Christlike *noblesse oblige*, for their loving Jesus and his people more than their own giftedness.

Earlier I described what is to me one of the most satisfying theological statements made in the twentieth century: the juxtaposition in Georges Rouault's *Miserere* of Plate 28, the one with the burial crypt representing the death of death in the death of Christ, and Plate 29, the one with the sunlit landscape representing the song that Christ's resurrection makes possible. Christ's death is but a doorway to resurrection, and Christ's resurrection means that each day is part of his great liturgy of song.

But the exquisite power of these two plates lies in the way they answer the plate they follow.

The plate just before these depicts the Greek musical hero, Orpheus. Lord of song though he is, Orpheus has failed to conquer death and bring his wife Euridyce from the underworld. Broken now, he kneels, magic lyre hanging silently from his side, his head lifted in resignation toward the gods, waiting death's blow himself. Beneath, Rouault has inscribed a line from Virgil: *Sunt lacrymae rerum*—"There are tears in things." Comment art critics Frank and Dorothy Getlein:

The bringer of music to mankind, one of the sweet conceptions
of the ancient, pre-Christian world, must, like the humblest wan-
derer in the world, bare his throat to the knife the world has always
ready for the cut. In this graceful resignation we see the highest
wisdom of the ancient world. We live in death's dominion and
must accept its doom.[29]

The power over death that the noblest art does not have, our
Singing Savior does have. Thus, just as Clement of Alexandria
pointed beyond Orpheus to Christ as God's own "New Song,"
so Rouault pushes past the dead end of classical antiquity to the
renewal of life and the return of song in Jesus Christ. Because of
his song, we do not end our journey with throats upturned in
lonely resignation; rather, we sing our way to a final destiny in
the City of God. And along the way, our song takes on a deeper
wonder and a grander wisdom because of the generations of artists—kissed by God's grace with gifts like Orpheus's—whom the
Singing Savior distributes among us.

9

Bubba's Voice

"'Tis the Gift to Be Simple"

"Tis the gift to be simple," begins the Shaker anthem. When we sing simple songs, we say something about a Savior who came as an artisan's son, worshiped in unadorned fashion, and took up with sinners like us.

Though his lineage was royal, Jesus's upbringing was anything but. By the standards of the refined Jerusalem elite, the Galilee of his upbringing had an embarrassingly high Bubba-factor. Raised in an artisan's home, God-in-flesh got dirt under his fingernails. His parables depicted God's kingdom in terms that debtors, day laborers, fishermen, and prostitutes could follow.

Jesus Sings Folk

Jesus's worship life was simple and unpretentious. Though his parents took him to the Jerusalem temple at least twice (at his eighth day and in his twelfth year) and perhaps annually (Luke 2:41), the posture he himself took toward the temple as an adult was altogether hostile. The Bible shows us Jesus characteristically worshiping in synagogues, not in the temple.

During Jesus's life, there was a marked split between temple and synagogue. The Sadducean temple aristocracy were patrons of the temple and therefore were custodians of the richly ornamented worship of the post-exilic literature. In the view of many, though they may have kept its form they had prostituted its spirit. Pharisees, by contrast, lived closer to "the people of the land" ('am-hā'āreṣ), and the worship they sponsored in the synagogues was aesthetically lean by comparison. Emerging apparently during Israel's and Judah's exiles, synagogues became centers more of prayer and teaching than of sacrifice and elegant liturgy. Synagogue music appears to have been more a matter of the chanting of texts than of instrumental atmospherics. Musicologists say the synagogue music of Jesus's day would have been more democratic and folk song-like, not marked by the professionalism of the temple with its trained musicians.[1] Moreover, I imagine synagogue worship would have been colored more by the reserved mood of Psalm 137, leaving the festive mood of Psalm 150 to temple worship.

"Bubba" has always described the sociology of Christ's followers. When Jesus's disciples became leaders of the Jerusalem church they were treated as country bumpkins. They were, after all, unschooled, ordinary men, notable only for having been with Jesus (Acts 4:13). From the portrait of Paul in Acts, we understand that the apostle to the Gentiles was himself a man of some upbringing. He was a citizen of both Rome and his native city Tarsus ("no

mean city," he insists), and he was educated in Jerusalem by one of
the leading rabbis of his day (Acts 21:39; 22:3, 27–28). Nonetheless, his letters show that he despised social snobbery. He chided
the Corinthian church for their elitism and challenged them to
see the focus of God's calling in the lowly among them:

> Brothers, think of what you were when you were called. Not many
> of you were wise by human standards; not many were influential;
> not many were of noble birth. But God chose the foolish things
> of the world to shame the wise; God chose the weak things of the
> world to shame the strong. He chose the lowly things of this world
> and the despised things—and the things that are not—to nullify
> the things that are, so that no one may boast before him.
>
> 1 Corinthians 1:26–29 NIV

In the latter half of the second century, it was precisely such
"scruffy" origins that the cultured pagan Celsus found so distasteful
about Christians. He called Christians a bunch of "wool-workers,
cobblers, and laundry-workers, and the most illiterate and bu-
colic yokels, who would not dare to say anything at all in front of
their elders and more intelligent masters."[2] According to Celsus,
Christians "show that they want and are able to convince only the
foolish, dishonourable and stupid, and only slaves, women, and
little children."[3]

So stinging was Celsus's critique that some seventy years later
(around AD 250) one of Clement of Alexandria's students, Origen, felt the need to respond with a defense of Christianity. In his
Contra Celsus Origen proudly acknowleged what Paul had said
about God choosing the lowly, but then Origen pointed out the
more urbane features of what Paul expected of bishops: that they
should be learned, prudent, and sensible (citing 1 Tim. 3:1–7).
We, asserted Origen, have rich and poor, cultured and uncultured:
the Word "makes all men worthy of God."

Indeed, part of the argument Origen and other Christian apologists mounted against the cultured despisers of the faith is that the classical tradition of paganism was the exclusive property of the favored. Despite its aspirations to bring *kalokagathia* ("the beautiful and good life") to humankind, in the end cultured paganism, they believed, was elitist and sterile. In Christianity, the "kindness and philanthropy of God" had come to high and low—to Bach and Bubba—alike, and made them brother one to the other.

The Folk Songs of the Church

No sooner had I embraced Christ, you will recall, than Mort Whitman enlisted me to play guitar in our church services. He picked the hymns, I wrote out the chords in my hymnal, and we intermixed hymns and folklike "praise songs" in our worship. At the same time, I started listening to all this beautiful classical music on my dorm room stereo. Curious as to how much of that kind of music had worked its way into our Presbyterian hymnal, I checked its index of composers.[4] To be sure, there was the occasional piece by Bach, Beethoven, Haydn, or Schumann. The names that dominated were lesser musical lights: Bradbury, Dykes, Mason, Sankey, to name a few. However, a surprisingly large amount of music came from "Anonymous" or "Traditional."

I imagine that, like ours, most churches' hymnals illustrate what Origen argued seventeen and a half centuries ago: the Word "makes all men worthy of God." Remarkably, the congregation of the Singing Savior sings both Haydn's "The Heavens Are Telling the Glory" and African American slaves' "Were You There?"

After just a few weeks of accompanying hymns on the guitar, I realized many hymns have a simple chord structure, and part of what makes them so singable is that on emphasized beats they stay around the tonic chord (C in the key of C), the subdominant (F in the key of C), and the dominant (G in the key of C). Then I began to notice that the chord structure of our hymns was frequently not different from that of our folklike "praise songs." The hymn "Holy, Holy, Holy" did not progress much differently than the praise song "I Am the Light of the World"[5]; it certainly was not any more challenging to play.

Several years later, friends at the Chapel Hill Bible Church introduced me to the music of the St. Louis Jesuits, composer-singers within the Roman Catholic folk mass movement.[6] I came to appreciate how similarly songs like Giardini's melody TRINITY (to which "Come, Thou Almighty King" is normally sung) and the Jesuits' signature folk hymn "Glory and Praise" and Bob Dylan's signature folk anthem "The Times Are A'Changin'" moved. Maybe it is just because I am an unreconstructed folk guitarist from the sixties, but it seems clearer to me as time goes by that many hymns are more enjoyable to *play* and *sing* than to listen to. When I sit down with a hymnal and a guitar there is a "back porch" feel that almost automatically attaches itself to songs such as "Guide Me, O Thou Great Jehovah"; "Come, Christians, Join to Sing"; and "Like a River Glorious."

Those early days of accompanying hymns and praise songs were my introduction to a reality I could not articulate until years later: congregational song is functional art.[7] It is music more "of the people" and "by the people," and less "for the people." Congregational song is participatory art, not performance art. Its power lies in the fact that we share it as a group rather than receive it from a recitalist. A lot of what we would call "art music" or "classical music" is beyond the ability of ordinary people. When it is done in worship, "art music" tends to be done by the few on behalf of the many. Bach's *Mass in B Minor* is a composite of many pieces (mostly orchestral and choral) and was never intended for congregational participation. Bach's *Passion According to St.*

Matthew and *Passion According to St. John,* lovely and powerful as they are, connected with their congregations because of how generously laced they were with hymns. Handel's *Messiah* was written for, and for years was performed only in, concert halls, not churches.

The logic of incarnation and redemption is one of God's accommodating himself to us; it is about his "stooping so low but sinners raising."[8] When he stoops he brings hymnody that connects us to him and to each other. Hymns have rightly been called by many the "folk songs of the church." Many hymns and folk songs are not musical masterpieces. Even so, they are not beneath the dignity of the Singing Savior, nor of those he calls his brothers and sisters. The music that has served the church most effectively over the long haul is simpler stuff, because the Singing Savior takes up Bubba's voice.

Wise classically trained musicians take care not to be so impressed with their idiom that they fail to appreciate how helpful it can be to mix music that is more familiar and more accessible, if humbler, along with music that is challenging and educational. They are aware that being taught the life story behind Bach's and Handel's work can be as valuable to a congregation as hearing the notes done correctly. Bubba prefers "Amazing Grace" and "When the Roll Is Called Up Yonder." However, the Bubbas among us may be able to receive Bach, if we're helped to understand how a piece like "Jesu, Joy of Man's Desiring" (or better, the original *"Jesus bleibet meine Freude"*) arises from an experience of Christ that is like our own.[9]

Similarly, wise "pop" musicians are careful not to disdain a perceived lack of artistry in folk songs nor dismiss the datedness of hymns, understanding that those features are exactly what make many hymns and folk songs work so well. Every so often a student at UNC/Chapel Hill would thank our worship planners for not neglecting older hymns: "They're important bridges to my upbringing." A seminary student of mine once was asked by a small Assembly of God congregation to help them with their worship. Being of charismatic background, he assumed he could bring his repertoire of songs from contemporary music publishers like the Vineyard, Integrity/HOSANNA!, and Maranatha, and things would be fine. For a couple of weeks, he played and sang pretty much by himself as folks politely listened. Then he decided he had better ask: "This doesn't seem to be working. What would *you* like to sing?" Their answer: old-time hymns. That was the day they started to find their groove.

Honest Music That Takes Us beyond "Tribalism"

Folk legend Pete Seeger's mother was a classical violinist. Classical music is what she wanted her son to like and play. His father was a musicologist, and as a boy Pete sometimes accompanied his father on expeditions to find new music to study. When Pete was sixteen he traveled with his father from their home in New England to Asheville, North Carolina, to take in a square dance and ballad festival. It was the younger Seeger's first exposure to folk music, and it was love at first hearing:

> I liked the rhythms. I liked the melodies, time-tested by generations of singers. I liked the words. Compared to the trivialities of the popular songs my brothers and I formerly harmonized, the words of these songs had all the meat of human life in them. They sang of heroes, outlaws, murderers, fools. They weren't afraid of being tragic instead of just sentimental. They weren't afraid of being scandalous instead of giggly or cute. Above all, they seemed frank, straightforward, honest. By comparison, it seemed to me that too many art songs were concerned with being elegant and too many pop songs were concerned with being clever.[10]

For Pete Seeger, frankness and honesty trump elegance and cleverness. And indeed, folklorists of the twentieth century such as John and Alan Lomax armed themselves with "portable recording machines" and began traveling the country in search of the "honest" music of the heartland—music that otherwise would never have found its way into concert halls or onto airwaves.[11] They inspired folk artists such as Pete Seeger and Woody Guthrie to keep those songs alive, and to produce new songs of like style. The result was a renewed interest in the latter half of the twentieth century in all kinds of folk music from all over the world.

But it is church—the place where the family of God sings its parlor songs—where the most honest music has thrived. When Fanny Crosby points to "blessed assurance" in Jesus, her own physical blindness lends to her credibility. Nor is it a shallow consolation Horatio Spafford claims when at the loss of his children at sea he confesses, "Even so, it is well with my soul." Here in the church are the frank and honest songs. The folk songs of the church create a climate of comfort and familiarity in which we can be real with one another about why we need a Savior.

The folk songs of the church also give shape to different truths and moods of the faith itself. Whatever stream of Christianity any of us has landed in—high or low Protestant, Catholic or Orthodox—we have received a heritage of song. Christian philosopher Nicholas Wolterstorff says we all have our "tribal" music.[12] There's incredible richness in the Christian family tree, and each branch seems to have been entrusted with a special insight and a unique voice.

Our spiritual forbears sensed a particular "fit" between their preaching of the faith and their singing of the faith. Lutheran chorales and hymns have their own way of interweaving the objectivity of Christ's work *for* us with the subjective benefits of his life *in* us. Methodist and Moravian hymns have theirs. Genevan metrical psalms embody both the *gravitas* (the weightiness) of what it is to worship a holy God, and the delight of having this holy God draw near in grace. Baptist testimony songs give voice to the Christian instinct for telling our neighbors the Good News, while Baptist hymns make their own contribution to Christendom's majestic praise. Anglo-Catholic settings of "service music" adorn worship that is a weekly recapitulation of the history of redemption. Orthodox chanting makes palpable the mystery of the interconnectedness between heaven and earth. The grittiness of spirituals (both African American and shape-note[13]) preserve the cross-shaped hopefulness of life lived out in pilgrimage. We're all trustees of a profound gift.[14]

Many communions, in fact, are learning musically what theologian Robert Webber has taught: ours is an ancient-future faith, and so, in many respects, the way forward takes us through the past. Respectful attention to heritage is a bridge to the future. Gregorian chant, for instance, seemed like a novelty when the recording *Chant* by the Benedictine Monks of Santo Domingo de Silo came out in 1994. But the flourishing since then of simple Taizé meditation songs is testimony to the desire of many for worship that feels at once rooted, mysterious, and familiar.[15]

My own tribe is the Calvinist. The clans within this tribe are numerous and enthusiastic—from exclusive psalm-singers to singers of psalms and (old school) hymns (in old school ways), to minstrels rewriting old school hymns with new folklike melodies, to progressives who self-consciously contextualize their singing to their regional or ethnic or demographic setting.[16] Our family homecomings are not always cordial. We have to keep reminding ourselves of what Paul told the Romans (if I may paraphrase): "One sings praise songs as well as psalms. Another abstains from praise songs and sings only psalms. Let not him who sings everything despise her who abstains, and let not her who abstains judge him who sings everything; for God welcomes him. . . . He who sings everything sings in honor of the Lord, since he gives

thanks to God. She who abstains, does so in honor of the Lord
and gives thanks to God. None of us lives to ourselves, none of
us dies to ourselves."[17] We have to learn to do what my friend and
colleague Steve Brown says the functional family does on long
vacations in the car—it bans the headphones and lets Grandma
and Junior take turns picking the family's music.

Christianity is an embodied faith, not a mere collection of
ideas and beliefs. While the gospel creates communities, its music
helps to knit those communities together. There is such a thing
as "mere Christianity," as C. S. Lewis once put it, an irreducible
core of beliefs and practices that will constitute a community as
Christian as opposed to something else. "A generous orthodoxy,"
as emergent church leader Brian McLaren calls it, is not less than
orthodox—it is measured by the Apostles' and the Nicene Creeds.
Nonetheless, the history of the church has produced a host of
ways communities can embody and sing the faith. Lewis likens
the acceptance of "mere Christianity" to entering "a hall out of
which doors open into several rooms." It's a grand thing to find
oneself in the hall, instead of outside in the cold.

> But it is in the rooms, not in the hall that there are fires, and chairs
> and meals. The hall is a place to wait in, a place from which to try
> the various doors, not a place to live in. For that purpose the worst
> of the rooms (whichever that may be) is, I think, preferable.[18]

Each of us finds ourselves in a community that has come from
somewhere and that does things certain ways for certain reasons.
We sing a particular song this way instead of that way. Our liturgy is shaped this way and not that. As each group develops its
nuances, it becomes a family and develops its own folk culture.
That's necessary, and it's good. But we say something profound
about the gospel itself when we stay a family and refuse to allow
ourselves to become insular, a closed-in group. By God's grace,
we can nurture the good we've inherited from our family tree,

further its contribution to the larger body of Christ, and at the same time appreciate—and perhaps learn from—folks who sing Christ's song differently.

Because of the communications revolution of the past century and a half, we are arguably in a better position than any prior generation to understand how we have come to sing Christ's song the way we have.[19] One of the greatest challenges of our day is to live with what sociologist Peter Berger calls "the heretical imperative," that is, an awareness that our tribe's way of embodying the faith is not the only option. As we become more aware of each other's song we see more clearly that our own way of singing is a choice. It's not the only option. None of us embodies wholly the wholeness of who our Savior is. In that realization we avoid the pitfalls of what we might call xenophobic "tribalism"—the belief that the gospel stands or falls with the particular way in which *our* tribe sings it.

Moving beyond tribalism calls for a certain temperance about the way we hold to our particular traditions. Because he loves the people he is called to serve, a psalm-singing colleague of mine forces himself to sing the hymns and praise songs of our seminary's chapel services, and he goes out of his way to tell me he appreciates what we do musically. In like vein, a student from a hymn-singing background told me the other day how "blown away" he was when he experienced metrical psalm-singing for the first time at a conference he attended: "I had no idea how powerful it could be to sing the Word of God. It was worshipful and beautiful and surprisingly easy."

Ours is a world that communication and commerce have made quite small. Contrary to modernist visions of world harmony, the closeness has made living together more difficult, not less. Tribalism is not on the wane, as suicide bombings in crowded streets, genocide in countrysides, and jet planes flown into skyscrapers attest. It's a time to stand against evil, but also a time to sing alongside brothers and sisters whose voices are just different—different

perhaps even by virtue of belonging to another clan of our own
tribe—but not necessarily thereby wrong. This is one of the most
significant ways we signal to "the powers and principalities in
the heavenly places" what is "the manifold wisdom of God" who
has made into family members those who once were aliens and
strangers to one another as well as to God.[20]

Music That Teaches the Grace of Humility

I've argued that Bubba-music is Jesus's music; in the first place,
because Jesus himself came in lowly fashion; in the second place,
because at the center of God's electing love are "the lowly things
of this world and the despised things—and the things that are
not." Third, I've tried to show how this lowlier music helps to
shape us into communities of worship.

There is one more consideration I would like to put before us
on behalf of the simpler songs: they teach us the grace of humility.
C. S. Lewis recounts his early days as a Christian:

> When I first became a Christian . . . , I thought that I could do it
> on my own, by retiring to my rooms and reading theology, and
> wouldn't go to the churches and Gospel Halls; . . . I disliked very
> much their hymns which I considered to be fifth-rate poems set
> to sixth-rate music. But as I went on I saw the merit of it. I came
> up against different people of quite different outlooks and differ-
> ent education, and then gradually my conceit just began peeling
> off. I realized that the hymns (which were just sixth-rate music)
> were, nevertheless, being sung with devotion and benefit by an
> old saint in elastic-side boots in the opposite pew, and then you
> realize that you aren't fit to clean those boots. It gets you out of
> your solitary conceit.[21]

I confess to having my own snobbery. I would like to think it
is musical snobbery, but I cannot dignify it that way. My musical

aesthetic is self taught, so I rely on the judgment of others for real artistic judgments. No, my snobbery is social. Some brands of music simply suggest sociologies I do not care for. While some music is "down home" enough to make me feel comfortable, some is, to me, superficially "down home" and puts me in mind of a big-hair, leisure-suited, flashy-toothed disingenuousness that makes me embarrassed. But the fact is, those folks are a part of me, and so is their music.

The Gaithers have been good for me. Since the 1960s Bill and Gloria Gaither have been at the forefront of bringing Christian music to a mass audience, and they have been strong advocates of hymn singing. They believe hymns anchor our faith. Suggests Gloria, "A hymn like 'Great Is Thy Faithfulness' offers . . . stanzas that recount our history with God, that move our hearts to offer the praise expressed in the chorus."[22] Moreover, the Gaithers are known for their "Homecomings," in which they feature the Southern gospel singing of their own roots. In their "Homecomings" not only do the Gaithers do homage to the musical forms that shaped them, but they pay loving tribute to the men and women who taught them the music. I have to work hard to love this kind of music—but love it I do, because I know Jesus loves the people who sing it.

The church is "home" for believers. Folklike music and simple hymns make the church feel like a place where you belong. The apostle Peter recognizes that believers are a "holy nation" (1 Peter 2:9), but he emphasizes that together they make up a household (1 Peter 2:5)—and the ethic he lays out for them is that of a home. Peter's special concern is that people at the lower end of family life—in his day, slaves and women—understand how transfigured their roles are because of Christ, who himself came as a suffering servant. By speaking to relationships between husbands and wives and masters and servants, and by doing so in terms altogether recognizable from their social world, Peter calls his readers to an experience of family. Interestingly, the first word he uses to describe them is "elect" (NIV): they are brothers and sisters in a family not of their own choosing (1 Peter 1:1).

When we submit to the song of Bubba among us, we say "Yes!" to the Savior who has called us into his family and who sings among us his hymn to the Father.

10

THE BLUES BROTHERS' VOICE

"On a Mission from God"

One of my teenage sons has set out to play the electric guitar. He's chosen the "masters" of the instrument to be his instructors. When I come home from work I'll hear him in his bedroom playing along with Jimi Hendrix, Stevie Ray Vaughan, or Deep Purple.

I asked my son what he thinks it means to do "contemporary music." "You do what Eric Clapton did," he said. "Clapton learned the blues by studying Mississippi Delta Blues greats like Son House and Robert Johnson. Clapton put the great players inside himself. Then he became 'present' to his audience. He didn't try so much to take his audience back to Son House, but to bring Son House to his audience. Yngwie Malmsteen did the same thing. He grew up loving Bach's chord progressions and melodies. When he was in his early teens he discovered the nineteenth-century violin virtuoso Nicolo Paganini. Malmsteen learned the electric guitar by learning Paganini. And then he took the music that had shaped his soul to the people of his own 'heavy metal' generation. What came out of his Stratocaster was a unique kind of neoclassical rock. Both Clapton and Malmsteen were (and are) very much *contemporary* musicians in that they connect to audiences of the present. Although they mastered music of the past, they never devolved into mere imitation or regurgitation."

Like the Blues Brothers who went "on a mission from God" to bring their band together and save the orphanage that raised them, we are "on a mission from God" to help our generation and those that follow to find their own voice in the Savior's song. Singing the Blues Brothers entails caring about the world in which we live, immersing ourselves so deeply in the way the song of redemption has been sung by our forebears that we intuit how to sing it in our own day.

Music critic Martha Bayles captures a Blues Brothers sense of contemporaneity in her phrase "extroverted modernism," which to her is an attitude toward art that is "neither aggressively radical nor arrogantly dismissive of tradition," that seeks to relate "to life as it is actually lived—not just by the privileged few, or by artists, but by everyone," that "doesn't feel compelled to defy popular taste or to overestimate art that is inaccessible to ordinary people," and that "does not make the mistake of making art into a religion."[1] As examples of the "extroverted modernism" she approves she points to the way Picasso rooted his cubist experiments in the draftsmanship he had studied in the academy, to the way Manet and the impressionists refused to stop caring about popular acceptance, and to the way early rock and roller Chuck Berry claimed: "I was trying to shoot for the whole population instead of just . . . shall we say, the neighborhood?"[2]

The theology of the Bible exudes similarly confident connectedness with its intended readership. The sun and the moon were deities in pagan pantheons. When in the creation account Moses refers to them merely as two "great lights" without even naming them, he communicates to an understanding readership that the sun and the moon are but created luminaries that serve their Creator's purposes.[3] David wants God's people living in a land once given to the worship of nature gods to understand that it is Yahweh, not the Canaanite Baals, who is Lord over the storm: "Yahweh thunders over the mighty waters . . . the voice of Yahweh breaks the cedars" (Ps. 29:3, 5).[4] Jesus portrays the radical nature of "neighbor love" by imagining a hated Samaritan caring for a half-dead Jew who has been left to perish by his countrymen. Paul is not content to leave his theological heirs with just his theology of faith, hope, and love. He provides Timothy and Titus with manuals to help their churches articulate and embody a faith that is understandable to pagan contemporaries who value ancient Greek virtues like "godliness, justice, self-mastery, and courage" but do not have the resources to attain them.[5]

The Bible can take this posture because of its confidence in its grand story line: the Bible tells of a Savior who has claimed our world and all its tomorrows as his own. New Testament scholar Oscar Cullmann compares Jesus's resurrection to D-day.[6] When the Allied forces established a beachhead at Normandy, World War II was over. The rest was essentially a mopping up exercise. To be sure, Berlin was still a long way off. The Battle of the Bulge lay ahead. But the Normandy beachhead signaled that the Allied forces were too strong not to prevail. Likewise, the Bible treats the resurrection of Jesus Christ as firstfruits of a harvest that cannot help but come in, and as a down payment or a deposit on a final settling of accounts that God is determined to execute.

Because of Jesus's resurrection, New Testament theologian George Ladd says, we live in "the presence of the future."[7] Of the era in which we live since the coming of God in the flesh, C. S. Lewis says: "Among times there is a time that turns a corner and

everything this side of it is new. Times do not go backward."[8]
Between now and when Jesus returns to usher in the age to come,
Paul provocatively quips, "all things" are ours (1 Cor. 3:22–23).
I suggest this includes the music of whatever generation we live
in, because, as Paul continues, "we belong to Christ, and Christ
belongs to God."

Because the future has come to us in Jesus, we are called to go
to the nations that he, their rightful King, is reclaiming through
the good news of his kingdom. The New Testament shouts its
confidence: "This . . . was not done in a corner," Paul tells Agrippa
(Acts 26:26 NKJV). Early Christians felt themselves grasped by
something that demanded an allegiance higher than blood ties
and regional loyalty. Like Paul, they were impelled to go to the
corners of the earth and tell everybody that eyes could be opened,
that it was possible to turn from darkness to light and from the
power of Satan to God (Acts 26:18). They believed God would go
with them to the dark, demon-controlled places. They believed
that in their message, in their lifestyle, and in their worship, Christ
was singing among the nations (Rom. 15:9). There is an "outward-
boundness" to the gospel that a faithful church will not neglect
to incorporate into its worship.

I'm asked from time to time, "Why can't we just use the musical
language of the accumulated Christian culture and let the world
learn to sing *our* way?" My answer is to point to what God has
done for us in Christ. The early Christians' outward-boundness
is a reflection of God's own heart, for Jesus came to take God's
song to the nations.

Jesus's Outward-boundness

God's song among the nations is evident in Jesus's ministry.
Matthew elegantly bookends his Gospel with the pilgrimage of
the Magi "from the East" at the beginning (chapter 2) and the

Great Commission ("make disciples of all the nations") at the
end (chapter 28). Matthew centers Jesus's ministry in Galilee, and
he does so for more than biographical reasons. To be sure, the
Galilee of Jesus's upbringing and ministry is on the traditional
northern frontier of Israel. However, Matthew sees in Galilee a
theological frontier as well, noting that Isaiah had called it "Galilee
of the Gentiles":

> The land of Zebulun and the land of Naphtali, the way of the sea,
> beyond the Jordan, Galilee of the Gentiles—the people dwelling
> in darkness have seen a great light, and for those dwelling in the
> region and shadow of death, on them a light has dawned.
>
> Matthew 4:15, citing Isaiah 8:23

Luke too shows us Christ's passion for the nations. He observes
that the offense that Jesus's Nazarene neighbors (and how many
must have been at least distant kin?) take at him is his pointing
beyond their provincial dreams to God's interest in Sidonians
and Syrians:

> "I tell you the truth," he [Jesus] continued, "no prophet is accepted
> in his hometown. I assure you that there were many widows in
> Israel in Elijah's time, when the sky was shut for three and a half
> years and there was a severe famine throughout the land. Yet Elijah
> was not sent to any of them, but to a widow in Zarephath in the
> region of Sidon. And there were many in Israel with leprosy in the
> time of Elisha the prophet, yet not one of them was cleansed—only
> Naaman the Syrian." All the people in the synagogue were furious
> when they heard this.
>
> Luke 4:24–28 NIV

In order to remind Israel of her Abrahamic call to be a light
to the nations, Jesus ministers along the Mediterranean coast
(in classical Sidonia) and in the Decapolis of the Golan Heights

and beyond (in classical Syria). The New Testament's outward-boundness is grounded in Jesus's own heart for the nations; and his heart beats to a theme deeply embedded in the ancient vision of the Hebrew Scriptures.

Koine Greek and Musical Koine

One of the more subtle ways the New Testament demonstrates its confident outward-boundness lies in the language in which it is written. Since many people think of music as a kind of language, the shape of the Bible's language can be instructive for our attitude toward song.

With not the slightest hint of self-consciousness, New Testament writers—all of them—laid out their thoughts in the Greek of their audience rather than in the Hebrew of their faith's deepest roots. They chose to use not the heritage language of Israel but the universal language of the world into which they were being sent.

Centuries later Europeans noticed how different the Greek of the New Testament was from classical Greek, and many concluded that the New Testament had been written in a secret, in-house "Holy Ghost Greek." It was not until non-literary papyri started being unearthed in the nineteenth century that scholars began to realize that the New Testament's linguistic world was much more ordinary. Indeed, New Testament Greek is not, for the most part, literary and refined. It is certainly not the language of Homer, Demosthenes, Plato, and Aristotle. Nor is it, however, Greek of some sort of closed codebook, the secret dialect of a house turned in on itself. Rather, it is Greek that is contemporary and outward-bound. It is called "common Greek," Koine (the Greek term *koinē* means "common"). New Testament Greek's greatest resemblance is to the Greek of everyday life: of letter-writing, of novels, of bills and receipts, of ethical instruction manuals, even of graffiti.

Churches and artists who express their praise in the musical language of popular culture are following the example of the writers of the New Testament. "Nothing is more socializing than common speech; nothing more clique forming than jargon," contends Eugene Peterson.[9] Early Christians saw God building a church, not putting together a clique, and so they reached out with common speech. When Christians today worship God in musical Koine, whether they realize it or not, they are following the same script.

I'm asked on occasion, "When we use what you call musical Koine, don't we inevitably have to whittle the gospel down to the size of the music of popular culture or, worse, buy into its assumptions? Doesn't the medium taint the message?"

Nobody who asks me this is ever protesting the simplicity of "Amazing Grace." They're always talking about whatever song too comfortably reflects popular culture for them at the time— whether "Shine, Jesus, Shine" from the 1980s or "Shout to the Lord" from the 1990s or "Undignified" from the new millennium. It's the Blues Brothers they're worried about, not Bubba. What they mean is: Doesn't the musical medium of rock and roll, born in the 1950s and popularized in the rebellious teen culture of the 1960s, inevitably trivialize our message and compromise Christ?

The question has two dimensions, actually. One has to do with the music's sophistication (or lack thereof). The other has to do with the music's moral worth (or lack thereof). For both dimensions of the question, I point again to the language of the New Testament.

First, the choice of Koine Greek did not mean a "dumbing down" of the message, a capitulation to the limitations of Bubba. Though in the main it is a rather humble medium, the language of the New Testament conveys sublime truths. In fact, if it had seemed important to New Testament writers to make sure the vessel was worthy of its cargo, precedent was already at hand, because a movement for a return to the more cultured Greek of Aristotle's day had already emerged by the first century. Philo of Alexandria (20 BC to AD 50) was writing Jewish theology in ultra-elegant and ultra-difficult classical Greek. And by the end of the first century, the Jewish historian Josephus had editors help him upgrade his Greek for his refined Roman audience. Christians too would eventually strive to rise above the crudity of Koine. Clement of Alexandria (mid-third century) wrote in complicated, elegant classical Greek, as did Eusebius of Caesarea, court historian of the first Christian emperor, Constantine (mid-fourth century).

From the first to the fourth century, the Mediterranean world saw something of a literary purge. A lot of first century Greek literature simply was lost or destroyed because it was deemed substandard. Fortunately, because of their revered status, the New Testament writings survived. Clearly, the reason for the New Testament's status is that despite its literary commonness, what it had to say was so compelling, and its various ways of saying it were so profound, that replacing it was unthinkable.[10] In their outward-boundness, New Testament writers stood against the elitist flow.

Second, whatever worldly and godless associations rock and roll has as a musical language, they pale beside the promethean aspirations of Koine Greek's principal benefactor, Alexander the Great. Koine Greek (a simplified Greek made up largely of Attic and Ionic elements) became the common language of the Mediterranean world because of Alexander's military and cultural imperialism. Alexander's army and administration were held together by a flattened out Greek that both infantry grunt and provincial governor could speak. Moreover, Alexander's minions imposed their language along with their purportedly superior Hellenistic way of life on proud and indigenous cultures.[11]

Perhaps we should be amused at the way God used a product of Alexander's militarism and the pseudo-gospel of Greek culture to spread the liberating and truly good news of Jesus's kingship. So maybe we can relax a bit and acknowledge that despite the pretensions of some in the 1950s and 1960s to create a new music that would unite a generation in overthrowing traditional morality and politics, this music and its progeny continues even now to unite generations in praise of the living God. A gospel that is centered in the story of One who became like us "in every way, yet without sin" bears within itself a statement of the ability of the divine to take to itself the human, "in every way, yet without sin." The New Testament's use of Koine Greek is a case in point.

Moreover, when we take a closer look at the New Testament itself, we can see how diversely contoured a "common" or "popular" cultural medium can be and how demanding its craftsmanship can be as well. Despite the fact that the New Testament seldom approaches the formal elegance or complexity of classical authors, its voicing has an extraordinary richness of range.

Mark is probably the least elegant; if anybody is writing in a second language it is he. Greek writers liked to use subordinate clauses. Mark uses them less frequently than Matthew and Luke, the other synoptic Gospel writers. His sentences are simpler, though a little more awkward. Even so, and despite the fact that his version of a given story tends to be wordier and less polished than Matthew's or Luke's, Mark provides the crispest, liveliest, and most focused overall narrative of Jesus's life. That's why he uses the adverb "immediately" so much, and why he slips into the historical present tense so frequently. For instance, though none of the translations renders it this way, Mark 1:12 literally reads: "And immediately the Spirit drives him into the wilderness."

John's Gospel has been called "shallow enough for a baby, deep enough for an elephant." The child who is just mastering "See Dick. See Jane. See Spot" can handle "The Word was with God, and the Word was God" (John 1:1 NKJV). Despite his syntactic minimalism, however, John is the New Testament's theological maximalist. Nobody shoots higher than "Before Abraham was, I AM" (8:58 NKJV).

Then, in the book of Revelation, this same John turns around and paints his apocalyptic visions with a rule-bending surreal Greek, necessitated by the mind-bending reality shown him. The phrase "from him who is and who was and who is to come" reads too nicely in English (Rev. 1:4 NASB). In Greek it is a monstrosity—because its doxology is of colossal proportion. "Who is" and "who is to come" are fine. John uses participles with definite articles in conventional fashion: literally, "the being one" and "the coming one."[12] John wants to say the same thing about the Lord's preexistence—the fact that he always "was." And John wants to say it in parallel fashion. The problem is that Greek (like English) has no past participle of the verb "to be"; the language just does not do, "was-ing." But John does not want to break the article-verb pattern, so he says: "the was one,"[13] a turn of phrase that is just as awkward in Greek as it is in English.[14] As if to anticipate twentieth century surrealists, John adopts modes of expression that demand a second, closer look. He seems to be saying, "If you want to see things for what they really are, forget about the way your eyes have worked until now."

Luke has one of the New Testament's more refined literary hands. Occasionally he turns phrases that let you know what a sophisticate he is. His formal prologue addressed to "most excellent Theophilus" (Luke 1:1–4) shows him to be "a conscious littérateur of the Roman period," to borrow a phrase from commentator Joseph Fitzmyer.[15] When he and Paul are shipwrecked on the island of Malta, Luke reports, "The natives [literally, 'the barbarians,' which means 'non-Greek speakers'] showed us no small kindness" (Acts 28:2). When he narrates the gospel's expansion toward Rome, he tends to use the infinitive as a gerund according to the rules of classical Greek syntax: "A soothsaying slave girl's meeting us took place as we were going to the place of prayer," would be a closer rendering of Acts 16:16 than those the translations provide. However, when Luke recounts the events of Jesus's life, he foregoes the infinitive that Greek style calls for and lets his narrative read like the rougher translation Greek of some portions of the Septuagint: "And it came about in those days that a decree went out from Caesar Augustus that all the world should be enrolled" (Luke 2:1).[16]

Paul's hand is profoundly functional. He can pitch things as high as he needs to—or as low. He and Luke are the only writers ever to quote classical writers.[17] Paul protests that he refuses to use rhetorical devices, all the while making devastating rhetorical points. His arguments are elaborate, his images vivid and sometimes embarrassingly earthy: he says he counts the credentials of his past life as so much *skubala*, a Greek term that is just about as crude as a four-letter English word that, like it, means "excrement" (Phil. 3:8).[18] Paul almost singlehandedly invents the epistle as pastoral tool. You can envision him bending the medium to serve his message, trying with the size of his closing signature to overcome the distance that necessitates his letter-writing: "See with what large letters I am writing to you with my own hand" (Gal. 6:11 NASB).

Now, it should not go unnoticed that God does press into service a more Philo-like, a more elegant and classical hand in the epistle to the Hebrews. Here Jesus is the "radiance of the glory of God" and the "exact imprint of his nature"—that's as rarefied a set of expressions as the New Testament offers (Heb. 1:3 ESV). Readers of the Greek text of Hebrews are readily aware that they have entered a distinct literary world within the New Testament. This document has always served as a precious pointer to a more philosophical and elevated way of conceiving Christian truth. As such, however, Hebrews is notable for two features: first, for its being exceptional in the New Testament canon; second, for the spanking it administers to those whose literacy and sense of cultural heritage mask spiritual infancy: "Though by this time you ought to be teachers, you need someone to teach you the elementary truths of God's word all over again" (Heb. 5:12 NIV).

"The medium is the message," runs Marshall McLuhan's famous dictum. Arguably, there are dimensions to the reality of Christ that Bach embodies better, that Bubba embodies better, and that the Blues Brothers embody better. But Christ is Christ. If we believe he lives beyond the grave to press home his case to the human race through the power of the Spirit, then we believe he is Lord over what and how he communicates. He stands above classical culture, above folk culture, and above popular culture. He is able to morph to his own shape all the different media he touches. God did not shortchange himself when he chose the earthen vessel of Koine Greek to deliver the most important message he has ever sent to the human race. Nor do his people shortchange him when they respond with the music of their Koine.

As a linguistic collection, the New Testament stands as a profound embodiment of God's intent to press his life into ours. The person of Christ, McLuhan once offered, "is the only case in which the medium and the message are perfectly identical."[19] It's extraordinary the way this union of medium and message is carried over into the New Testament itself. God modeled his passion for the world by pressing into service the medium of Koine Greek. He dignifies with his own worth whatever vessel he chooses. There is a profound carryover for us as we think about how we sing.

As God's incarnate love, Christ reached down to us with the hand of royalty. Musically, therefore, he takes up Bach's voice among us to unite us in song that is elegant and refined. As God's embodied life, Christ reached down to us with work-blistered artisan's hands. Musically, therefore, he takes up Bubba's voice to unite us in song that is homespun and intimate. As God's compassion walking on the earth, Christ grabs us with an insistent hand and joins our hand to our neighbor's. Musically, therefore, he takes up the voice of the Blues Brothers to unite us in song that is simultaneously rooted, fresh, and neighborly.

A Community of Voices

The New Testament itself is a community of voices in which the Savior speaks in both singular and multiple fashion. He builds his church by creating communities that share this characteristic. The New Testament incarnates the fact that a popular culture medium is not necessarily flat and one-dimensional.

What I have loved about my years at Northland is the New Testament–like range of voices within its musical Koine. Bach and Bubba are not regulars at Northland's services; the Blues Brothers are. Unfortunately, some devotees of contemporary worship music clearly despise classical and folk music. For my friends at Northland, however, the heavier use of popular music is more a matter of gauging what is the musical heart-language of the congregation. Bach does show up from time to time. And occasionally, there's an "all request" worship service: Bubba always takes center stage those Sundays. For the most part, though, this church is more Koine, more Blues Brothers. But it is far from a monotone Koine, because sitting around its worship planning table are some voices that sound like Paul, some like the John of Revelation, some like the John of the Fourth Gospel, some like Mark. Refinement, functionality, surreality, profundity, and crispness all mark the voices of the Singing Savior's Koine in this community.

At a worship planning meeting, one voice suggests the hymn "Thou Who Wast Rich beyond All Splendor" as a lovely statement of the Savior's grand condescension. Another suggests it would juxtapose nicely with "Lord, I Lift Your Name on High."

Yet another says that song reminds him of a Richard Baxter quote of which he cannot imagine the song's composer was unaware.[20] The next thing you know, the elements are seamlessly woven together, with phrases from the Baxter quote projected as a motif connecting elements of a larger musical set.

At another meeting, one voice contributes an Afro-Cuban percussive groove to "O the Deep Deep Love of Jesus." Another asks whether the Great Thanksgiving Prayer of Hippolytus might shape this service's celebration of the Lord's Supper. Yet another voice composes an "Our Town"-inspired series of monologues to complement a preaching series on key lives from the book of Acts (Stephen, Barnabas, etc.). One more voice creates visuals to complement a solo of Twila Paris's "What Did He Die For?" Each person has a distinct set of preferences for what ideal worship would look and sound like, and the preferences are not harmonious at every point. However, everybody submits to one another's sense of what best serves the congregation's worship.

What makes it work is the belief that each voice is necessary and that each voice needs the other. What makes me love it is that it is biblical koinonia—friendship rooted in a common calling in Christ.

My point is not so much to defend a specific style of music. Nor do I offer guidelines for the use of a specific musical voice or the blending of several. There are all kinds of ways to mix Bach, Bubba, and the Blues Brothers. At the same time, it's quite possible to appreciate each voice in its own right. As John Calvin said (and might have better applied to this issue), "Charity is the best judge of what tends to hurt or to edify: if we allow her to be guide, all things will be safe."[21]

I hope I have said enough to make clear my fondness both for art music and folk music—the voices of Bach and Bubba. I will say that I believe the music my former teacher and now colleague John Frame has championed under the heading "contemporary worship music"—the voice of the Blues Brothers—has brought some worthy features to worship in the church of our day: God-centeredness, scripturality, freshness, and communicablity.[22] In my opinion, the African and Latin percussive sensibilities that have increasingly characterized American pop music can be profoundly enriching.[23]

I've noticed that worship songs that come from so-called "praise and worship" sectors are inclined to address God in the second person. This is a refreshing complement to hymns that more often (though not exclusively, of course) sing about God in the third person. Pastor John Piper rightly argues that though praise choruses are often musically simple, many of them articulate a hunger for transcendence.[24] While hymns are rather linear and content-laden, and while linearity and content are good, praise songs are more modular (focused on a single idea) and directly affective. Modularity and affect have their own virtue. It is simply off task to critique a praise song for not being a hymn. The power of any particular praise song has a lot to do with what it is teamed up with. To my mind, craftsmanship in worship design has as its first task the wedding of "right brain" and "left brain" elements, largely through the juxtaposition of thoughtful hymns and expressive choruses.[25]

Music That Teaches Generosity of Spirit

The last fifteen years have put me in Blues Brothers circles. I've been surprised at how hard I have had to work to learn its craftsmanship. It's been my observation that contemporary music is surprisingly more difficult to execute than one might think from hearing it on the radio or in concert. My innate rhythmic sense is more easily attuned to the squared off meters of classical music, folk songs, and standard hymnody. Despite years of choral and folk singing, I've found it challenging to learn to sing with an appealing pop sound. However, even more surprising than the rigors of the music of popular culture—and far more important—is the particular virtue the Blues Brothers have taught me. If Bach has taught me greatness of soul, and Bubba has taught me humility of heart, the Blues Brothers have taught me generosity of spirit.

One day several years ago, a student named Casey asked me to listen to some "alternative" praise music by a band he loved. I found it harsh and unappealing, so I asked him what the music did for him. "I love its intensity. Too much of the music we do in my church makes me yawn. It's safe and boring. It doesn't remind me that Jesus is bold and that life with him is adventurous. What I like about this music is that it sets my spirit on fire the way the gospel does." I never have been able to bring myself to care for the music of the group Casey liked. But I decided to consider whether Jesus was asking me to ponder this brother's attraction to a bolder and more intense musical expressiveness. I began to listen for what there is about "edgier" music that fires the spirit of people like Casey.

Over time, I came to appreciate what was at stake for people who are accustomed to a more percussive feel or to more elaborate rhythms in their music. Syncopation, a backbeat,[26] and other rhythmic devices can lend songs a richer, more pleasing texture. I found myself listening with their ears for the "bite" of the electric guitar; I realized it wasn't much different than the lift other folks get when an organist improvises, and modulates into the last verse of a big hymn. In a word, I found myself making room in my musical world for them. I feel I'm the richer for it, and I think it has pleased the Savior.

It's striking the way Paul closes his magisterial epistle to the Romans with this simple appeal: "each of us is to please his neighbor for his good, to his edification . . . accept one another" (Rom. 15:2, 7 NASB). The Blues Brothers have taught me to listen for Christ in the song of the "other."

CODA

"Join in This Choir"

The first community of Christians we know of who self-consciously related to Jesus as a Singing Savior was the church in Syrian Antioch, the place where believers were first called "Christians" (Acts 11:26). This ancient church produced a set of psalm-like songs that have come to us under the title *The Odes of Solomon*.[1] This congregation envisioned Jesus singing in their midst through their songs. They imagined him chanting a new song and "lifting his voice towards the Most High and offering to him those who had become sons through him" (*Ode* 31:3–4).

About AD 117 on his way to martyrdom in Rome, Ignatius, their great bishop and pastor, showed how deeply these songs had penetrated his theology, when he wrote to the Ephesians, "In your concord and symphonic love, Jesus Christ is sung." Accordingly, Ignatius invited believers, "join in this choir, that being symphonic in your harmony, taking up God's melody in unity, you may sing in one voice through Jesus Christ to the Father."[2] When seen in the light of this early dual vision of Christ singing in the midst of his people and of his people responding in "symphonic harmony," all our ongoing squabbles over how to do it right—which group's aesthetic will be honored, and which group's dishonored—take on their true measure.

Despite every attempt we make to pare his song list down to a manageable repertoire, Jesus is constantly expanding it. In the face of our careful attention to which niche market can be served by which vocal bandwidth, the Singing Savior is distributing his magnificent voice across an increasingly wide spectrum of musical idioms. In defiance of congregations' insistence on dividing themselves along age and affinity lines, Jesus teaches his people to defer to one another. Thus he blends the songs of generations and nations and families and tribes and tongues to make sweet harmony to the Father.

Jesus's voice is what counts, not ours; and his voice in "the great assembly" is as rich and complex as the constitution of his people. There is a unity and diversity in the voices of his assembly that we would not be able to hold together on our own. Then again, he has not left us on our own. If we but give ourselves to the concord and harmony of his love, as Ignatius says, Jesus Christ will be sung. Or rather, we will find we can hear "a real" and maybe not so "far-off hymn" being sung by the Savior himself.

Rather than play Bach, Bubba, and the Blues Brothers off one another—or even to hymn the virtues of each—my desire is to point us all to Christ and to urge us all to strain to hear his voice, one Ezekiel characterizes as being "like the sound of many waters," in the great multitude that Revelation says is itself "like the sound of many waters" (Ezek. 43:2; Rev. 19:6 NASB). If it pleases Jesus to distribute his voice among a wide range of singers and musical dialects, it would profit us to accommodate our preferences and principles to his.

Author Fyodor Dostoevsky found Jesus in the poor and suffering of Siberia. It is King Jesus's identification with his people in Matthew 25 ("I was hungry and you fed me") that gave Dostoevsky the warrant to articulate it this way. But he was only able to see Jesus there because he went there himself. Siberia was Dostoevsky's school of sacramental presence. In his own impoverishment and suffering among the Siberian outcasts, Dostoevsky learned to see Jesus.

It would be a wonderful thing if we all could put ourselves in a position to hear Christ's singular voice in the many voices of the people with whom he identifies. I cannot tell you how you might do this for yourself. I can, though, offer you three stories of how it has happened for me.

One spring in Chapel Hill, we decided to ask the choir to sing the "Crucifixus" from Bach's *Mass in B Minor* for the Maundy Thursday service. We underestimated the piece's complexity for our singers. In rehearsing the piece, we found that no vocal line seemed to have any logic at all. Every part felt as if it was on some torturous meandering that defied all sense of purpose and betrayed no congruence with anything else. There was murmuring. About two weeks before Maundy Thursday, though, something magical happened. We got it. Suddenly, the crushing dissonances connected with one another, and rehearsal nearly came to a blubbering halt—not out of frustration, for once, but out of a shared sense of the exquisite horror of what Bach's music portrayed. Never have I felt more connected to "the fellowship of Christ's sufferings" and to brothers and sisters who share the hope of life in him. I heard the Singing Savior that night, and he was singing Bach.

On another North Carolina evening I sat among prison inmates as part of a ministry team from our church. I always feel small in a jail or prison. That night, I found myself thinking about "Fred," and this made me feel especially small. I had never gotten to know Fred well. But when I first moved to Chapel Hill he would stand during open prayer times in church and pray for the men he ministered to in jail. His words were clumsy and his mannerisms were awkward, but Fred's love for the inmates he visited each week was evident. One day several years ago he was picked up by some fellows who were rather like the men he had been reaching out to in prison. They took Fred down a side road, tied him to a tree, savaged him, and left him to die. None of the men sitting here had even known Fred, as far as I knew. Still, I felt small, because the distance between us seemed so great. I felt inadequate to the task of reaching out to these men with the kind of love that Jesus had for them and that Fred had tried to bring them. Then an inmate took hymnals out of a cabinet, passed them around, and said something like, "How about we start with 'Power in the Blood'?" There followed hymn after hymn telling the story of Jesus's love for sinners and thanking the Father for "strength for today and bright hope for tomorrow." I had been in similar settings before: there is nothing—nothing—like jailhouse hymn-singing. It is as though the earth itself is crying out for release. Because of my reflections on Fred, though, I was surprised by its poignancy that night. The distance melted, and Jesus sang Bubba in our midst.

One weekend at Northland when I was scheduled to lead worship, the planning team decided to use a particular praise song I cannot abide but which has enjoyed wide currency in contemporary worship circles for some time. I have tried to articulate musical reasons why I think the song is unworthy of use: "It's Christian kitsch. It's trite." However, friends with lots more training than I respond with a "You've got to be kidding" look. During one of the weekend's services, I noticed in the front row a young lady next to an older woman. They looked enough alike that I figured them to be daughter and mother. I knew the younger was a regular. But the older was clearly a first-time visitor; she spent much of the service looking around, as though she were trying to get her bearings. It was easy to see the nervousness in the daughter's body language too. I found myself feeling her unease: "Will Mom like this? Will she approve?" Then we got to the song I do not like. Suddenly, the mother's resistance visibly melted; she turned and embraced her daughter, as if to say, "Now I see why this place means so much to you." And they clung to each other as they sang, tears streaming from both sets of eyes. I was undone too. I saw the "solitary conceit" of my assumptions about the shallowness of the song and of the people who would like it. Though I had not recognized it at first, Jesus had been connecting the generations using music I thought was too "common" for his service. Turns out, I got to hear him singing the Blues Brothers.

As I mention in the preface, one of my heroes is Edmund P. Clowney. As president of Westminster Theological Seminary from 1966 to 1982, he boldly carried the banner for a faith that is rigorous and challenging and true. And as *Christianity Today*'s original "Eutychus and His Kin" columnist and skillful poet and hymn writer, Clowney showed how artfully and imaginatively one can think theologically.[3] Another former student of Clowney's, Bill Edgar, testifies:

> Ed was concerned that the great poetry of God's love had not sufficiently been felt in the fabric of church life. He wanted us to know that in worship angels were present. In the church's outreach there is a joyful gathering up, a theophanic parade to Zion. And there is singing. He was quite funny about how no one ever asked him to sing a solo. But he believed Christ to be the great choir master, directing even the most tone-deaf in a heavenly chorus of praise and adoration.[4]

An article Clowney wrote entitled "The Singing Savior" sent me to the Scriptures to gasp for the first time at this wonderful dimension of who my Savior is.[5] In many respects, this book pays tribute to Clowney for the way he pointed many of us to a Christ

who sings his love to his bride. Accordingly, it's only right that
Clowney should have the final say:

Their mighty song burns heavenward and glory shines in
  sound;
The herald angels praise the Lord in shouts that shake the
  ground.
O sing, you sons of heaven's joy, the wonder of his ways;
The birthcry of an infant boy perfects his Father's praise.

O sing, dear Jesus, Mary's son, let pilgrim songs ascend;
How great the works the Lord has done, his mercies without
  end!
O sing in Nazareth, young man, the songs of jubilee;
Today fulfill redemption's plan, proclaim the captive free!

O sing, my Savior, lift the cup, "Jehovah is my song!"
The sacrifice is offered up before the shouting throng;
"I come to do your will, my God. My body is prepared
To drink the cup and bear the rod that sinners should be
  spared."

O sing, Lord Christ, up Zion's brow from Kidron's rocky bed;
The pilgrim songs are silent now, and all your friends have fled.
Yes, sing in agony, my King, the God-forsaken Lord;
And count your bones in suffering while malice mocks your
  word.

Then sing, ascending King of kings; lift up your heads, you
  gates;
The King of Glory triumph sings, the Lord that heav'n awaits.
O sing, you Son of God's right hand, our Prophet, Priest, and
  King;
The saints that on Mount Zion stand, with tongues once dumb,
  now sing.

O sing, Lord Christ, among the choir in robes with blood made
    white,
And satisfy your heart's desire to lead the sons of light.
O Chief Musician, Lord of praise, from you our song is found;
O Ancient of eternal days, to you the trumpets sound.

Rejoicing Savior, sing today within our upper room;
Among your brothers lift the lay of triumph from the tomb.
Sing now, O Lamb, that we may sing the glory of your shame,
The anthem of your suffering, to sanctify your Name![6]

NOTES

Chapter 1 "A Red Guitar, Three Chords, and the Truth"

1. Bono, Introduction to *Selections from the Book of Psalms* (New York: Grove Press, 1999), ix.

2. Genesis 4:21. For more on Jubal, see chapter 8, pp. 138.

3. Exodus 15:1–21 for the song at the Red Sea; Deuteronomy 31:30–32:43 for the song that precedes the crossing of the River Jordan.

4. See 2 Samuel 23:1, where David is described as "the man raised up as the ruler chosen by the God of Jacob, Israel's beloved singer of songs" (NET Bible). This last phrase, *ne'îm zamîrôt yiśrā'ēl*, means something like the sweetness (or pleasantness or loveliness) of the songs of Israel, yet most translators consider it to be a description of David himself, in parallel with his being God's champion (*haggéber*) and messiah (*mešî'ḥ*). David is Israel's ruler and the embodiment of her rich life of song. My rendering as "Sweet Singer of Israel" is a conflation of NASB's, NKJV's, and ESV's "sweet psalmist of Israel" and NET's "Israel's beloved singer of songs." The conflation was suggested to me by James A. Michener's use of it in *The Source* (New York: Random House, 1965), 263.

5. Ibid., 257 (in general, the chapter "The Psalm of the Hoopoe Bird," 199–273).

6. For the complementary portraits of David as "Sweet Singer" and as Architect of Praise, see chapter 3.

7. For God's glory cloud at the temple dedication, see pp. 69 and 2 Chronicles 5:11–14. Second Chronicles 20:14-25 narrates Jehoshaphat's sending singers "out before the army" of Judah. At their song, the Lord "set ambushes against

the sons of Ammon, Moab, and Mount Seir, who had come against Judah; so they were routed" (v. 22 NASB). Isaiah promises that beyond her exile as punishment for sin, Judah will experience a new exodus and a new song in celebration thereof (e.g., 42:10–13; 43:1–7). Similarly, Zephaniah looks beyond Judah's exile to her return to Jerusalem where Judah sings with joy and God sings over her with love (3:14–20).

8. Mary's Magnificat, Luke 1:46–55; John the Baptist's and Jesus's respective contradictions of people's expectations, Luke 7:31–35. From the medieval carol "Tomorrow Shall Be My Dancing Day" to Steven Curtis Chapman's "Lord of the Dance," believers have sung of Jesus's incarnation and redemptive mission under the metaphor of a "dance." Justification for doing so lies in the cryptic terms of the proverb Jesus introduces at Luke 7:31–32: "To what then will I compare the people of this generation, and what are they like? They are like children sitting in the marketplace and calling to one another, 'We played the flute for you and you did not dance; we wailed, and you did not weep.'" If I may unpack the explanation that follows: No, Jesus had not come (though John the Baptist had) to sing a prophetic jeremiad and to weep over how awful sinners were (v. 33). Instead, Jesus had come to start the dance of deliverance for gluttons, drunks, tax collectors, and sinners; and the "righteous people" should have been playing their flutes to accompany his dance (vv. 34–35). For examples of the way Israel's psalms anticipate Jesus's identity in Matthew's Gospel alone, see Matthew 13:35—Psalm 78:2; Matthew 21:9; 23:39—Psalm 118:26; Matthew 21:16—Psalm 8:2 (and compare Matthew 11:25); Matthew 22:44—Psalm 110:1. Jesus sings a hymn before going to the Mount of Olives, Matthew 26:30.

9. Paul sings hymns in prison, Acts 16:25. Paul's instructions to sing, Ephesians 5:19; Colossians 3:16 (see note 1 in chapter 2). On the matter of the hymnic nature of Paul's writing, see pp. 111.

10. I have merged texts from several versions, with that printed in Joseph Hillman's *The Revivalist* (1868) serving as my baseline; Anne Warner's original lyrics are ca. 1864. Noel Paul Stookey performs it on his 1979 *Band & Bodyworks* (Neworld Media). Enya does a two-stanza version on her 1991 *Shepherd Moons* CD (Time Warner). Tim Manion, formerly of the St. Louis Jesuits, does a three-stanza version on his *There Is a River* (Phoenix: North American Liturgy Resources, 1985). The melody is by Rev. Robert Lowry (ca. 1864). Doris Plenn added the verse—"When tyrants tremble sick with fear"—to honor friends imprisoned during the McCarthy period (Peter Blood-Patterson [ed.], *Rise Up Singing* [Bethlehem, PA: A Sing Out Publication, 1988], 43).

11. Most singers know the last line as "Since love is Lord of heaven and earth, how can I keep from singing?"

12. *How Can I Keep From Singing: A Northland Worship Album* (Northland foundation for the Arts CD 0100-2 © 2000).

13. "How Can I Keep From Singing," *eva by heart* (Blix Street Records CD G2-10047 © 1997).

14. See Mark Pinsky, *The Gospel According to Disney: Faith, Trust, and Pixie Dust* (Louisville: Westminster John Knox Press, 2004), 1.

15. David Kelsey, *The Uses of Scripture in Recent Theology* (Philadelphia: Fortress Press, 1975).

16. See the chapter "Apologetics: From Rationalism to Embodiment," in Robert Webber's *The Younger Evangelicals: Facing the Challenges of the New World* (Grand Rapids: Baker, 2002), 94–106.

17. Bob Dylan, "Pressing On," Special Rider Music (© 1980), recorded by Dylan in 1980 on *Saved* (Columbia CD CK 36553), and by the Chicago Mass Choir in 2003 on *Gotta Serve Somebody: The Gospel Songs of Bob Dylan* (Columbia CD CK 89015). All rights reserved. Used by permission.

18. Reported by Mark Pinsky, "Have Bible, Will Rock," *The Orlando Sentinel*, April 5, 2003, E1.

19. Bono, Introduction to *Selections*, x, xi.

20. "All Along the Watchtower," U2, *Rattle and Hum* (Island CD 422-842 299-2 © 1988).

21. Anne Lamott, *Traveling Mercies: Some Thoughts on Faith* (New York: Pantheon Books, 1999), 46, 48.

Chapter 2 The Psalms

1. See Colossians 3:16; Ephesians 5:19. Concerning what Paul means by "psalms, hymns and spiritual songs," I follow the general schematization laid out by Donald P. Hustad, *Jubilate II: Church Music in Worship and Renewal* (Carol Stream, IL: Hope Publishing Co., 1981, 1993), 146–148. Hughes Oliphant Old provides a profitable discussion of the way Old Testament psalms underlie the emergence in the New Testament of Christian psalmody (e.g., Mary's song in Luke 1:46–55) and hymnody (e.g., Paul's hymn to Christ in Colossians 1:15–20) (*Worship: Reformed According to Scripture* [Louisville: Westminster John Knox Press, revised and expanded 2002], 36–39). In an unpublished article ("Song in Worship: the Fruit of the Richly Indwelling Word of Christ"), Edmund P. Clowney contends, and I think rightly so, that by "spiritual songs" Paul means not only Spirit-prompted exclamations but also songs the church composes that are expressive of the "wisdom and spiritual insight" toward which Paul prays in Colossians 1:9.

2. Eugene Peterson, *Answering God: The Psalms as Tools for Prayer* (San Francisco: Harper Collins, 1991).

3. David Crowder, "I Need Words," © 2002 by Six Steps Music/worship together.com songs. All rights reserved. Used by permission..

4. As cited in Nancy L. deClaissé-Walford, *Reading from the Beginning: The Shaping of the Hebrew Psalter* (Macon, GA: Mercer University Press, 1997), 33.

5. For this insight I am indebted to Mark Futato, in conversation and in *Transformed by Praise: The Purpose and Message of the Psalms* (Phillipsburg, NJ: P & R Publishing, 2002).

6. For this, see deClaissé-Walford, *Reading from the Beginning*, 34. In Books One through Three, she counts fifty-two "laments" and twenty-four "hymns"; in Books Four and Five, thirty-seven "hymns" and fifteen "laments." The classification is standard—see William H. Bellinger, Jr., *Psalmody and Prophecy*, JSOT Supplement Series 27 (Sheffield, UK: JSOT Press, 1984).

7. In outlining the flow of the Five Books of the Psalms, I borrow variously from students of the shaping of the canonical Psalter: chiefly Futato, *Transformed by Praise*; and deClaissé-Walford, *Reading*; but also William L. Holladay, *The Psalms through Three Thousand Years: Prayerbook of a Cloud of Witnesses* (Minneapolis: Fortress Press, 1993); and Gerald H. Wilson, *The Editing of the Hebrew Psalter*, SBLDS 76 (Chico, CA: Scholars Press, 1985).

8. Paul Elie, *The Life You Save May Be Your Own: An American Pilgrimage* (New York: Farrar, Straus and Giroux, 2003), x.

9. The image is from Charles Frazier, *Cold Mountain* (New York: Vintage Books, 1997). The call to a systematic reading through the Psalter is from Eugene Peterson, *Answering God*.

10. William L. Holladay, *A Concise Hebrew and Aramaic Lexicon of the Old Testament* (Grand Rapids: Eerdmans, 1971), 76.

11. Eric Werner, "Jewish Music," *New Grove Dictionary of Music and Musicians*, 9:623; the Mishnah citation is B. Megillah 32a; see Edward Foley, *Foundations of Christian Music: The Music of Pre-Constantinian Christianity* (Collegeville, MN: Liturgical Press, 1996), 55.

12. Peterson, *Answering God*, 26.

13. See, for example, 1 Samuel 20:36–37.

14. Peterson, *Answering God*, 25.

15. For acrostics see Psalms 9–10; 25; 34; 37; 111; 112; 119; 145.

16. Peterson, *Answering God*, 24.

17. G. K. Chesterton, *Orthodoxy* (London: L. Jane, 1912).

18. Per Joy Patterson's setting in *The Presbyterian Hymnal: Hymns, Psalms, and Spiritual Songs* (Louisville: Westminster/John Knox Press, 1990), no. 194.

19. *Psalter Hymnal* (Grand Rapids: CRC Publications, 1987, 1988), no. 105, "Trumpet the Name! Praise Be to Our God!" I'm grateful that Seerveld was able to reduce nineteen metrical verses to nine, largely through a witty conflation of the ten plagues that includes the line "fish dead and frogs in Pharaoh's bed."

20. Hart is Director of Worship at Grace Episcopal Chuch in Orange Park, Florida, and fellow faculty member of Robert Webber's Institute of Worship Studies.

21. For a sample of Simplified Anglican Chant, go to <http://www.reg giekidd.com>. Other examples of Simplified Anglican Chant are available in *The Hymnal 1982 Service Music: Accompaniment Edition Volume 1* (New York: The Church Hymnal Corporation, 1985), S408–S415. A little more difficult, but lovely and powerful nonetheless, are the eight psalm tones by Hal Hopson in *The Book of Common Worship* (Louisville: Westminster/John Knox Press, 1993), 598–783; with other canticles and ancient hymns, 573–591. Pete Seeger once quipped, "Let the altos lead," meaning group singing needs to be done at a lower pitch these days, since fewer people have trained voices. Accordingly, when I use the Hopson tones in public worship, I set all but one of them (Tone 5) to a lower pitch. Tone 1 I lower by a half step; Tones 2, 3, 4, 6, and 8 by a whole step; and Tone 7 by a minor third. Another fine resource for chant is the two-volume work by Carl P. Daw, Jr., and Kevin R. Hackett, *A HymnTune Psalter*, Book One, *Gradual Psalms: Advent through the Day of Pentecost*, and Book Two, *Gradual Psalms: The Season after Pentecost* (New York: Church Publishing Inc., 1998). For psalms prescribed by the Episcopalian lectionary, Daw and Hackett offer a hybrid of chanted verses, and refrains based on familiar hymn tunes.

22. M. W. Smith © 1981, 1986, Meadowgreen Music.

23. Chris Tomlin, "Forever," © 2000 by Six Steps Music/worshiptogether .com songs. All rights reserved. Used by permission.

24. Compare Matthew 5:5 with Psalm 37:11–12.

25. Vinnette Carrol, Alex Bradford, Micki Grant, *Your Arms Too Short to Box with God* (ABC Records © 1977).

26. de Classié-Wolford, *Reading from the Beginning*, 103; James Limburg, *Psalms* (Louisville: Westminster/John Knox Press, 2000), 493–94; Alan Harman, *Psalms* (Geanies House: Christian Focus Publications, 1998), 22, 446; G. H. Wilson, *The Editing of the Hebrew Psalter* (SBLDS, 76; Chico, CA: Scholars Press, 1985), 220–28—Wilson notes that these psalms, in addition to being the great doxology of the Psalter, present Yahweh as the mighty and eternal King, in contrast to the weakness of human kings portrayed in Psalms 2–89; Futato, *Transformed by Praise*, 14.

27. Text and story in Ulrich S. Leupold (ed.), *Luther's Works*, vol. 53, *Liturgy and Hymns* (Philadelphia: Fortress Press, 1965), 211–16.

28. Kemper Crabb, "Warrior," © 1982 Fifth Monarchy Music (admin. by Music Services). All rights reserved. ASCAP. Used by permission.

29. Caedmon's Call covered the song on *In the Company of Angels—a call to worship* (MMI Essential Records CD 83061-0621-2 © 2001).

Chapter 3 David

1. Baruch Halpern, *David's Secret Demons: Messiah, Murderer, Traitor, King* (Grand Rapids: Eerdmans, 2001), 6.

2. Ibid., chapter 3, "Dating 2 Samuel." Halpern is probably correct in arguing that the preservation of the stories was affected by infighting over whether the throne should be Solomon's. As son of David's choice, Solomon would have had no small interest in people seeing David's life in a sympathetic light.

3. See Childs's discussion of the emergence of the psalm titles and their application to David as representative man in "Psalm Titles and Midrashic Exegesis," *Journal of Semitic Studies*, vol. 16/2 (Autumn 1971), 137–50.

4. The events to which these psalms are keyed are as follows: 1 Samuel 19:11 (Psalm 59); 1 Samuel 21:11 (Psalm 56); 1 Samuel 21:13 (Psalm 34); 1 Samuel 22:1 (Psalm 142); 1 Samuel 22:9 (Psalm 52); 1 Samuel 23:19 (Psalm 54); 1 Samuel 24:3 (Psalm 57); 2 Samuel 8:13 (Psalm 60); 2 Samuel 12:13 (Psalm 51); 2 Samuel 15:16 (Psalm 3); 2 Samuel 15:23 (Psalm 63); 2 Samuel 16:5 (Psalm 7); 2 Samuel 22:2–51 (Psalm 18).

5. Pierce R. Pettis III, "Absalom, Absalom," © 1996. All rights reserved. Used by permission.

6. Named Shimei, according to 2 Samuel 16:5, or Cush, according to the title to Psalm 7.

7. Michener, *The Source*, 314.

8. Bono, Introduction to *Selections*, xi.

9. Ibid., x.

10. And also, according to 2 Chronicles 11:20–21, father of Maacah, Rehoboam's second wife.

11. Some, like Richard Pratt (*1 & 2 Chronicles* [Evangelical Press, 1997], ad loc.), say David is the singer (as do most translations). Some, like Mark Futato (per email correspondence, November 5, 2003), say that since the passage recounts Asaph's commissioning, it is more natural to understand Asaph as the singer. Some, like Eric Meyers (per email correspondence, November 3, 2003), suggest that 1 Chronicles 16:8–36 is not a repeat of what was sung in the service but a composition inserted by the chronicler that demonstrates the

legacy of psalmody passed on to Asaph. Personally, I think the text means that David or Asaph or both sang; thus, the conclusion of the song: "Then all the people said, 'Amen,' and praised the LORD" (v. 36 NASB). But I don't think the text forces a choice between David or Asaph. At the same time, the narrative resumes at 16:37 by reporting, "So he left Asaph and his relatives there before the ark of the covenant of the LORD to minister before the ark continually" (NASB). The "he" is clearly David. The fact that the text is content to use the pronoun at this point instead of naming David may imply that the narrator expects us to understand that David has been in view throughout the song just narrated. Still, the point is not beyond dispute.

12. It is not that the earlier portrait is being denied or suppressed; presumably, since the Samuel/Kings story has been told and is available to the reader, it does not have to be repeated. See 1 Chronicles 9:1; 2 Chronicles 20:34; 24:27; 25:26; 32:32; 33:18; 35:27; 36:8.

Chapter 4 Psalm 22

1. In this, I follow the analysis of Derek Kidner, *Psalms*, vol. 1 (Downers Grove, IL: InterVarsity Press, 1973), ad loc.

2. Puzzlingly, the NIV, the RSV, and the ESV translate this as the verb "save" or "rescue." This is strange simply because the root 'ānā' means "answer." Compounding the difficulty, these translations employ the same imperative mood as the verbs that precede it: "deliver me . . . save me." But unlike the preceding verbs, this one is in the perfect tense; it describes what God has done, not what David wants him to do. The NASB correctly translates the verb as descriptive, "You answer me." However, by keeping it with the prepositional phrase in front of it, and eliminating the "and" that precedes the preposition "from," the NASB presents a confused picture: "From the horns of the wild oxen You answer me." No, David asks to be rescued from the lion's mouth and from the horns of the wild oxen. God does so, and David almost incredulously exclaims: "You-answered-me!" In my view, the verb is rightly set off with its own line in the NKJV. See Peter C. Craigie, *Word Biblical Commentary*, vol 19. *Psalms 1–50* (Waco: Word Books, 1983), 200; Hans-Joachim Kraus, *Psalms 1–59: A Continental Commentary*, trans. by Hilton C. Oswald (Minneapolis: Fortress Press, 1993), 298; Allan Harman, *Commentary on the Psalms* (Fearn, Scotland, Gleanies House: Christian Focus Publications, 1998), 123. Harman notes that he follows the NIV marginal translation, "You answered me."

3. Psalm 16 offers the kind of prayer offered in the fulfilling of such a vow.

4. As expressions of such "neighbor-love," the Law had required that fields not be gleaned to their corners, that rest be provided every seventh day, that

cloaks not be taken as security, and that Levites get their share of the people's tithe (see, for example, Exodus 22:21–25; 23:9; Deuteronomy 5:12–15; 14:27–29; 24:17–22).

5. For example, "For when I bring them into the land flowing with milk and honey, which I swore to their fathers, and they have eaten and are satisfied and become prosperous, then they will turn to other gods and serve them, and spurn Me and break My covenant" (Deuteronomy 31:20 NASB). Deuteronomy's warning finds its counterpart in Luke's fool who says to himself, "Soul, you have many goods laid up for many years to come; take your ease, eat, drink and be merry" (Luke 12:19 NASB), and Luke's rich man whose luxurious laze juxtaposes so starkly to Lazarus's impoverished piety (see Luke 12:16–21; 16:19–31). In the same vein, Paul equates covetousness with idolatry and warns against those whose gods are their bellies (Ephesians 5:5; Philippians 3:19; see also Romans 16:18).

6. Though translations universally render this line, "You anoint my head with oil," the Hebrew idiom is more concrete, using the piel of the root *dāshēn*, "to make fat."

Chapter 5   Jesus's Lament of Abandonment

1. Chesterton, *Orthodoxy*, 138.

2. Ibid., chapter 8.

3. Edmund P. Clowney, "The Singing Savior," *Moody Monthly* (July-August 1979), 41.

4. On Rouault, see William Dyrness, *Rouault: A Vision of Suffering and Salvation* (Grand Rapids: Eerdmans, 1971—the quote is from p. 16, but the entire monograph bears out the thought; Hans Rookmaaker, *Modern Art and the Death of a Culture* (Wheaton: Crossway, 1994), 156–57; Gene Edward Veith, Jr., *State of the Arts: From Bezalel to Mapplethorpe* (Wheaton: Crossway, 1991), 166–74. The most accessible work in English that reproduces images displaying the range of Rouault's work is José María Faerna, *Rouault*, translated from the Spanish by Alberto Curotto (New York: Cameo/Abrams, Harry N. Abrams, Inc., 1997).

5. Georges Rouault, *Miserere* (Paris: Editions Le Léopard d'or, 1991), Plate 46. Note Gene Veith's comments on Plate 46, in *State of the Arts*, 172–73.

6. The music is available in *A New Hymnal for Colleges and Schools* (New Haven: Yale University Press, 1992), no. 266.

7. Found on *William Schuman: Violin Concerto* (HNH International Ltd. © 2001).

8. "Holy Darkness," © 1988, 1992, 1999, Daniel L. Schutte. Published by OCP Publications, 5536 NE Hassalo, Portland OR 97213. All rights reserved. Used with permission.

9. See Gerd Theissen's treatment of 1 Corinthians 4:1–4 in his *Psychological Aspects of Pauline Theology* (Edinburgh: T & T Clark, 1987), 59–66.

10. Compare 1 Corinthians 15:9, written during Paul's third missionary journey, about AD 55; Ephesians 3:8, written during Paul's first (apparently) Roman imprisonment, in the early 60s; and 1 Timothy 1:15, written after his release, somewhere in the mid-60s.

11. Mark Robertson and Beaker, "Surely God Is with Us," on Rich Mullins and a Ragamuffin Band, *The Jesus Record* (Sony CD 69309 © 1998).

12. Stephen and Jonathan Cohen, and Andy Millar, "Friend of Mine," as reprinted in *The Rocky Mountain News*, April 26, 1999, A14, with correction April 27, 1999. A recording of the song appears as a bonus track on the CD *WOW 2000*, vol. 2 (EMI, Word, Provident, Sparrow SPD 1703 © 1999).

13. James Ward, "So His Honor," *Lamb and Lion* (Music Anno Domini, LP © 1979).

14. Bono and the Edge, "Yahweh," *U2//How to Dismantle an Atomic Bomb* (Universal International Music BV CD B0003613-00 © 2004).

Chapter 6 Jesus's Victory Chant

1. Luke Timothy Johnson, *Living Jesus: Learning the Heart of the Gospel* (HarperSanFrancisco, 1998), x.

2. Ibid., 5.

3. Luke 8:49–56; 7:11–17; John 11:1–45.

4. The Roman church had originated among Jews and proselytes who had heard Peter and the apostles at Pentecost in Jerusalem in the early 30s (Acts 1:10). But from the late 40s, Jews had been absent from Rome, having been banished by decree of Claudius (see, for instance, Acts 18:2; Suetonius, *Life of Claudius* 25.4; Orosius, *History* 7.6.15–16). Understandably, a movement that had enjoyed a strong Jewish presence began to take on a decidedly Gentile flavor. In the mid-50s, now that Claudius is gone, Jews are returning, and among them are a lot of Jewish Christians, as evidenced by the large number of Jews Paul greets there (Romans 16).

5. Romans 15:9 (ESV), citing Psalm 18:49 and 2 Samuel 22:50. See Richard B. Hays, "Christ Prays the Psalms: Paul's Use of an Early Christian Exegetical Convention," in *The Future of Christology: Essays in Honor of Leander Keck*, ed. Abraham J. Malherbe and Wayne A. Meeks (Minneapolis: Fortress Press, 1993), 122–36.

6. Charles Wesley, "O For a Thousand Tongues to Sing" (Public domain, 1739).

7. Every discussion of the hymnic nature of any writings in the New Testament has to be cautious in view of the facts that: (1) no New Testament writer self-consciously employs Greek conventions of style and meter; and (2) no independent examples of apostolic hymns have surfaced to which to compare the New Testament writings. Discussions are inherently impressionistic. E. J. Foley's judicious remarks on "Christological Hymns" is a good starting point for the investigation of the question: *Foundations of Christian Music: The Music of Pre-Constantinian Christianity* (Collegeville, MN: Liturgical Press, 1996), 73–74. For an introduction to the Pauline hymns in general, see the splendid monograph by Robert J. Karris, *A Symphony of New Testament Hymns* (Collegeville, MN: Liturgical Press, 1996), on whose work I am dependent for much of what follows. It seems to me that with respect to Paul the situation is this: either Paul incorporated portions of early Christian hymnody into his writings, or (as I think is more likely the case) his writing took on such a lyrical quality on its own that he himself became a principal inspiration for the emergence of hymnody in the early church.

8. See Philippians 2:5–11. The literature on this passage is vast. I have adapted the rendering and have more or less followed the poetic structure of J. D. G. Dunn, *The Theology of Paul the Apostle*, 282 (see the bibliography there). See Karris, *Symphony*, 42–62.

9. See Karris, *Symphony*, 63–91.

10. On 1 Timothy 3:16, see Karris, *Symphony*, 112–26.

11. I am following the analysis of the majority of modern commentators, e.g., George Knight, *The Pastoral Epistles: A Commentary on the Greek Text* (Grand Rapids: Eerdmans, 1992), 406–8; J. N. D. Kelly, *A Commentary on the Pastoral Epistles* (London: A & C Black, 1963; Grand Rapids: Baker, 1981), 180–81; and Karris, *Symphony*, esp. 165–68. With its unusual use of the future tense in a conditional clause, the third line vividly brings before the reader the scenario of Judgment Day—if on that day we deny him, we are without hope. The fourth line brings us back to the present with its prospect of faithlessness on our part, where we are certain to fail. Each of the previous lines has an "also" in the second clause, indicating that the "then" clause is a natural consequence of the "if" clause; e.g., if we die with him, then we live with him. The lack of an "also" in the fourth clause suggests that the faithfulness the Lord shows in the face of our faithlessness is a promise to preserve us despite our failings, rather than a threat to treat us as our failings merit. There are, of course, dissenting views: I mention but Walter Lock, *A Critical and Exegetical Commentary on the*

Pastoral Epistles (Edinburgh: T & T Clark, 1924), 96; and Gordon Fee, *1 and 2 Timothy, Titus* (Peabody, MA: Hendrickson, 1984, 1988), 250–51.

12. Samuel Terrien's *The Magnificat: Musicians as Biblical Interpreters* (Mahwah, NJ: Paulist Press, 1995) is a rich study of musical interpretations of Mary's song.

13. See Karris, *Symphony*, 142–57. Reluctantly, for the sake of space in this particular book I leave aside Peter's comments on baptism. It is of no small import that his doxology of Christ is wrapped around commentary on the significance of our baptism. For it is in the cleansing waters that Peter believes, just like Paul, that we become united with Christ in his death and resurrection.

14. See Karris's elegant treatment (*Symphony*, 142–57). With Karris, I think verses 18 and 22 are hymnic material, while 19–21 (which I have not included) are commentary.

15. See Harry Blamires, *The Christian Mind* (New York: Seabury Press, 1963), esp. chapter 8, "The Sacramental Cast."

16. Twila Paris, "For the Glory of the Lord," *For Every Heart* (Sparrow Records, © 1988).

Chapter 7 The Singing Savior's Many Voices

1. Jake Vest, "'Hip Ain't Where Arthritis Hurts Most," *The Orlando Sentinel*, February 14, 2004, H1.

2. Yael Israeli, "King David Playing the Lyre," in Irène Lewitt, editor/project coordinator, *The Israel Museum* (Jerusalem: Laurence King Publishing, 1995), 79.

3. Clement of Alexandria, *Exhortation to the Greeks*, chap. 1. Greek text and archaic English translation are available in G. W. Butterworth, *Clement of Alexandria*, Loeb Classical Library, vol. 92 (Cambridge, MA: Harvard University Press, 1919). For these passages—all from chapter 1—I offer my own translation.

4. Ibid.

5. Paul's imagery is worth amplifying: when Jesus ascended to heaven, he gave "gifts" so the whole "body" could build itself up in love (Eph. 4:7–16). Explicit in the context of Ephesians 4 are the gifts of apostles, prophets, pastors, and teachers. Implicit from elsewhere are the gifts of the proclamation of the Word, by which Jesus makes sinners of saints; baptism, by which he cleanses his bride (Eph. 5:26); the eucharist, by which he communes with his people (1 Cor. 10:16); and the songs, by which he enriches his Word (Col. 3:16) and makes the Spirit's wisdom penetrate our hearts with joyful thankfulness (Eph. 5:19–20).

6. Following the dating proposed by Alexander Nairne, *The Epistle of Priesthood* (Edinburgh: T & T Clark, 1913), especially 207; Philip E. Hughes, *A Com-*

mentary on the Epistle to the Hebrews (Grand Rapids: Eerdmans, 1977); F. F. Bruce, *The Epistle to the Hebrews* (Grand Rapids: Eerdmans, 1990); B. F. Westcott, *The Epistle to the Hebrews* (Grand Rapids: Eerdmans, 1952). Westcott sees the destination of the letter as most likely Palestine with the time period of "just before the breaking of the storm" (xlii).

7. Eric Routley, *The Music of Christian Hymns* (Chicago: G.I.A. Publications, 1981), 82.

8. As David Koysis notes, "The Genevan tunes are set to wonderfully irregular metres and the tunes themselves have a pronounced rhythmic intensity and modal flavour, making them sound more like Renaissance madrigals than conventional hymns" ("Introduction to the Genevan Psalter," <http://www. redeemer.on.ca/academics/polisci/psalter_intro.html>). This despite Calvin's desire for music that was not "light" or "frivolous," but "weighty" and "majestic"—see Charles Garside, *The Origins of Calvin's Theology of Music: 1536–1543* (Philadelphia: American Philosophical Society, 1979); John Witvliet, "The Spirituality of the Psalter: Metrical Psalms in Liturgy and Life in Calvin's Geneva," *Calvin Theological Journal* 32:2 (November 1997), 273–97; Paul Westermeyer, *Te Deum: The Church and Music* (Minneapolis: Augsburg Fortress, 1998), 153–60.

9. I've tried to provide a rough approximation to the incredible breadth of Psalm 22, where Jesus sings among Israel and the nations, the poor and the rich, and the departed and the unborn. My thinking has been shaped by two sources. First, I am taken by three New Testament metaphors of community, especially as outlined by social historian E. A. Judge: the church is "city of God" (*politeia*), "household of God" (*oikonomia*), and "society of friends" (*koinōnia*). See E. A. Judge, *The Social Pattern of Christian Groups in the First Century: Some Prolegomena to the Study of New Testament Ideas of Social Obligation* (London: Tyndale Press, 1960). Second, I notice that students of aesthetics tend to distinguish between classical art, folk art, and pop art. Nicholas Wolterstorff, for instance, distinguishes between "high art," "works of the tribe," and "popular art" (*Art in Action: Toward a Christian Aesthetic* [Eerdmans, 1980], 21–22). Ken Myers distinguishes between "high culture," "traditional culture," and "popular culture" (*All God's Children and Blue Suede Shoes: Christians and Popular Culture* [Crossway Books, 1989], e.g., 120).

Chapter 8 Bach's Voice

1. In his *Pop Culture Wars: Religion and the Role of Entertainment in American Life* (Downers Grove, IL: InterVarsity, 1996), William D. Romanowski provides a lucid and sobering account of the emergence of the divide between "high

culture" and "pop culture" in American life (see especially chapters 1–3, "Total Recall," "Religion and 'Worldly' Amusements," and "High and Low Culture Wars"). With Romanowski, I eschew an understanding of "high culture" as being either morally superior (as some of its elitist defenders contend) or irredeemably corrupt (as some of its populist antagonists maintain).

2. I am using the term "classical music" not to refer specifically to the music of the "classical period" of the late seventeenth and early eighteenth century (the era of Franz Joseph Haydn). Instead, I employ the term "classical music" (along with its synonym "high art music") according to its more general sense: in reference to music that is governed by aesthetic theory, is dominant in academic music departments, and has historically found its financial base in institutions of power, e.g., royal courts, the church, wealthy patrons, government.

3. Applied explicitly to God's Son in the New Testament at Hebrews 1:8.

4. Bargil Pixner argues, correctly I think, that the name "Nazareth" is formed with Isaiah 11:1's reference to the "Branch (netzer) of David" in view and that the designation "Jesus the Nazarene" likely refers to Jesus's membership in a clan of Davidic descendants who populated Galilee following the Babylonian deportation (With Jesus through Galilee according to the Fifth Gospel [Rosh Pina, Israel: Corazin Publishing, 1992], 13–19).

5. Daniel J. Boorstin, The Creators (New York: Random House, 1992), 436.

6. Jane Stuart Smith and Betty Carlson, The Gift of Music: Great Composers and Their Influence (Wheaton: Crossway, 3rd ed., 1995), 35.

7. The elimination of the distinction, for instance, between the notes c-sharp and d-flat.

8. Hubert Kupferberg, The Mendelssohns: Three Generations of Genius (New York: Charles Scribner's Sons, 1972), 132.

9. Ibid., 182.

10. Led by Arnold Schoenberg (1874–1951), "twelve-note serialist" or "dodeca-phonist" composers laid out notes in a series in which, once the original note was set down, all other notes within an octave range were used before returning to the original note. The desire was to take away any hierarchy of importance for any particular note. The effect was to eliminate a tonal center.

11. See Paul Hillier, Arvo Pärt (Oxford, NY: Oxford University Press, 1997). Hillier recounts Pärt's early use of serialism on pp. 30–31, 34–46; he describes the Credo on pp. 58–63.

12. Ibid., 63.

13. Philosophers' trend-setting ideas will eventually be depicted by artists and sung and played by musicians. Conversely, some philosophical instincts are

better portrayed, in my view, than explained—Sartre makes much more sense to me in his plays than in his discourses. A good reader on the place of aesthetics in philosophy is Albert Hoftstadter and Richard Kuhns (eds.), *Philosophies of Art and Beauty: Selected Readings from Plato to Heidegger* (New York: The Modern Library, 1964).

14. Agriculture and manufacturing also emerge among the unbelieving children of Cain: Jabal is father of those who dwell in tents and have livestock, and Tubal-Cain is forger of all implements of bronze and iron.

15. William Edgar, *Taking Note of Music* (London: SPCK, Third Way Books, 1986), 24.

16. See Theissen, *Psychological Aspects*, 59–66.

17. C. S. Lewis, "The Weight of Glory," *The Weight of Glory and Other Addresses* (San Francisco: HarperSanFrancisco, 2001), 2.

18. See Alistair Kee, *Nietzsche Against the Crucified* (London: SCM Press, 1999).

19. Jaroslav Pelikan, *Fools for Christ: Essays on the True, the Good, and the Beautiful* (Philadelphia: Muhlenberg Press, 1955).

20. Pelikan, "Confessional Orthodoxy in Bach's Religion," chapter 4 of his *Bach Among the Theologians* (Philadelphia: Fortress Press, 1986), 42–55; see also Paul S. Minear, "Bach and Today's Theologians," *Theology Today* 42.2 (July 1985), 201–10.

21. Pelikan, "Pietism, Piety, and Devotion in Bach's Cantatas," chapter 5 of *Bach Among the Theologians*, 56–71.

22. An opera about Matthias Grünewald's Isenheim altarpiece.

23. An opera about St. Francis of Assisi.

24. See Josef Pieper's discussion of "greatness of soul" or "magnanimity" in *Faith, Hope, Love* (San Francisco: Ignatius Press, 1997), 101. Aristotle calls magnanimity (*megalopsuchia*) a crown of the virtues (*kosmos tōn aretōn*); Aquinas uses the phrase (in Latin) at *Summa Theologica* II, II, 129, 4 ad 3.

25. I am especially fond of the recordings of Sir Georg Solti conducting the Chicago Symphony Orchestra, *Mahler: The Symphonies* (London 10-CD Set 430-804-2 © 1971, 1972, 1983, 1991 Decca Record Company).

26. For more on Mahler see Egon Gartenberg, *Mahler: The Man and His Music* (New York: Schirmer Books, 1979); Kurt Blaukopf and Herta Blaukopf, *Mahler, His Life, Work, & World* (New York: Thames & Hudson, 2000); and Stuart Feder, *Gustav Mahler: A Life in Crisis* (New Haven: Yale University Press, 2004).

27. Subcription information is available from Mars Hill Audio, PO Box 7826, Charlottesville, VA, 22906-7826; or <http://www.marshillaudio.org/>.

28. Smith and Carlson, *The Gift of Music*. I have also found Patrick Kavanaugh to be an able guide to the world of classical music: *The Spiritual Lives of the Great Composers* (Nashville: Sparrow Press, 1993); *Music of the Great Composers: A Listener's Guide to the Best of Classical Music* (Grand Rapids: Zondervan, 1996); and *The Music of Angels: A Listeners' Guide to Sacred Music from Chant to Christian Rock* (Chicago: Loyola Press, 1999).

29. Frank and Dorothy Getlein, *Georges Rouault's MISERERE* (Milwaukee: Bruce Publishing Co., 1964), 81.

Chapter 9 Bubba's Voice

1. See the discussion in Edward Foley, *Foundations of Christian Music: The Music of Pre-Constantinian Christianity* (Collegeville, MN: Liturgical Press, 1996), 48–66.

2. Henry Chadwick, *Origen: Contra Celsum*, trans. with introduction and notes by Henry Chadwick (New York: Cambridge University Press, 1953; reprinted with corrections, 1965), 3:55; see 3:44–58, esp. 3:48.

3. Ibid., 3:44.

4. *Trinity Hymnal* (Philadelphia: Great Commission Publications, 1961).

5. Lyrics, melody line, and chords to Jim Strathdee's "I Am the Light of the World," composed in 1969, can be found in Yohann Anderson's, *The Tune Book* (San Anselmo, CA: Songs and Creations, Inc., 1972, 2004), no. 1. Since the 1960s, Anderson has been a leading promoter of folk songs in evangelical circles in the U.S. He makes available a number of helpful resources for the leading of group singing through his company, Songs and Creations, Inc. (mailto:yosongs@aol.com; 800.227.2188; <http://www.songsandcreations.com/>).

6. St. Louis Jesuits material is available through Oregon Catholic Press (OCP Publications, P.O. Box 18030, Portland, OR 97218-0030; 800.548.8749; <http://www.ocp.org/>).

7. Hustad, *Jubilate II*, 22–42.

8. To borrow a phrase from Frank Houghton's modern hymn, "Thou Who Wast Rich beyond All Splendor," *Trinity Hymnal* (Philadelphia: Great Commission Publications, 1990), no. 230.

9. The standard English text associated with this chorale from Bach's Cantata No. 147 *Herz und Mund und Tat und Leben* ("Heart and Voice and Deed and Life") is by Robert Bridges (1844–1930). The poem "Jesu, Joy of Man's Desiring" marks quite a departure from the spirit and content of the original Saloman Franck libretto from which Bach worked. Bridges's imagery is florid and romantic. He has our souls "soar(ing) to uncreated light . . . striving still to Truth unknown, soaring, dying round thy throne." Bach's original, by contrast, stays

low to the ground. It's a simple expression of the believer's love for the Savior, straightforward Lutheranism warmed by evangelical piety. In the final chorale each crisp phrase builds to nouns that express Jesus's value to the believer (the English translation is mine):

> *Jesus bleibet meine Freude, meines Herzens Trost und Saft.*
> Jesus remains my joy, my heart's trust and nourishment.
> *Jesus wehret allem Leide, er is meines Lebens Kraft . . .*
> Jesus wards off all sorrow, he is my life's strength . . .
> *Meiner Augen Lust und Sonne, meiner Seele Schatz und Wonne.*
> My eyes' desire and sun, my soul's treasure and delight.
> *Darum laß ich Jesum nicht aus dem Herzen und Gesicht.*
> Thus, I'll not let Jesus from my heart and sight.

I hold no brief for the superiority of performing pieces in the original language. In the case of this song, however, I have found no singable translation of the Franck/Bach libretto. When I've done this chorale with a choir, we've sung the German and provided an English translation.

10. Pete Seeger, *The Incompleat Folksinger* (New York: Simon and Schuster, 1972), 13.

11. For a sampling of the literature, see Alan Lomax, *The Land Where the Blues Began* (New York: Pantheon Books, 1993), from which I derive the term "portable recording machines," which Alan says he and his father John were the first to use in recording folk music in the 1930s, p. xi; and Nolan Porterfield, *Last Cavalier: The Life and Times of John A. Lomax* (Urbana and Chicago: University of Illinois Press, 1996). For access to Alan Lomax's field recordings, *The Alan Lomax Collection*, go to <http://www.rounder.com/series/lomax_alan/>. In addition, a catalog of field recordings preserved by the Library of Congress is available at <http://www.rounder.com/index.php?id=series/loc.php/>.

12. Nicholas Wolterstorff, *Art in Action* (Grand Rapids: Eerdmans, 1980), 22 and note.

13. Shape-note music employs note-heads of varying shapes to indicate different pitches. It was widely used in American folk hymnody (often referred to as "white spirituals") from about 1800 to about the time of the Civil War.

14. Of singular help is the research of Erik Routley, especially his *The Music of Christian Hymns* (Chicago: G.I.A. Publications, 1981). See also Andrew Wilson-Dickinson, *The Story of Christian Music: From Gregorian Chant to Black Gospel* (Batavia, IL: Lion Publishing, 1992).

15. Information on and materials from the ecumenical Taizé community in central France are available at <http://www.taize.fr/>.

16. For an uncompromising call to exclusive psalmody see Michael Bushell, *The Songs of Zion: A Contemporary Case for Exclusive Psalmody* (Pittsburgh: Crown and Covenant, 1980, 1993). For exemplary tools for psalm-singing and hymnody, see the *Psalter Hymnal* (Grand Rapids: CRC Publications, 1987, 1988), the hymnal of the Christian Reformed Church; and *Cantus Christi* (Moscow, ID: Canon Press, 2002), the hymnal of Christ Church, Moscow, ID—noteworthy is pastor Douglas Wilson's spirited call for music and lyrics that "result in a true cultural antithesis," vii. For the resetting of old hymns, see the resources on the website of Reformed University Fellowship <http://www.ruf.org/sounds/sounds.htm> and the series of *Indelible Grace* CDs, produced by Kevin Twit <http://www.igracemusic.com/>. Churches in this theological tradition that stand out to me for creatively crafting communitarian music that is in tune with their regional, ethnic, and demographic settings are: Green Lake Presbyterian Church, Seattle <http://www.greenlakepc.org/>; New City Fellowship, Chattanooga, TN <http://www.newcityfellowship.com/> and <http://www.jameswardmusic.com/>; Christ Community Church, Franklin, TN <http://www.communityworship.com/>; Redeemer Presbyterian Church, New York, NY <http://www.redeemer.com/>.

17. I'm paraphrasing and contextualizing Romans 14:1–18.

18. C. S. Lewis, *Mere Christianity* (New York: Macmillan, 1943, 1978), 12.

19. Bill Moyers's *Amazing Grace* DVD; KET, The Kentucky Network's video *The Big Singing*, brings to life the history and ongoing legacy of Billy Walker's 1834 shape-note songbook, *The Southern Harmony*.

20. See Ephesians 3:10 in the context of chapters 2 and 3 as a whole.

21. C. S. Lewis, "Answers to Questions on Christianity" from *God in the Dock: Essays on Theology and Ethics* (Grand Rapids: Eerdmans, 1970), 61–62. Thanks to Vernon Rainwater for calling my attention to this quote.

22. Mark Allen Powell, "There's Something About This Man," *Christianity Today* (April 2004), 34.

Chapter 10 The Blues Brothers' Voice

1. Martha Bayles, *Hole in Our Soul: The Loss of Beauty and Meaning in American Popular Music* (New York: The Free Press, 1994), 52–54.

2. Ibid. For Picasso, see p. 52; for Manet and the impressionists, p. 53; and for Berry, p. 148.

3. Though the point could be copiously documented, I mention but *Spirit of the Reformation Study Bible* (Grand Rapids: Zondervan, 2003), 8.

4. In similar fashion, Isaiah attributes to Israel's covenant Lord what Babylonia (where Israel's exile would take her) claimed for Marduk, e.g., to know

the future—see the extended polemic in Isaiah 46–48. The book of Proverbs points to Yahweh as the source of wisdom that Egyptians had thought to come from their gods (see Proverbs 22:17–24:22).

5. See Reggie M. Kidd, "Titus as *Apologia*: Grace for Liars, Beasts, and Gluttons," *Horizons in Biblical Theology* 21.2, December 1999, 185–209; with the editor's kind permission, available online at <http://www.reggiekidd.com>.

6. See Oscar Cullmann, *Christ and Time: The Primitive Christian Conception of Time and History* (London: SCM, 1951).

7. See George Eldon Ladd, *The Presence of the Future: The Eschatology of Biblical Realism* (Grand Rapids: Eerdmans, 1974).

8. C. S. Lewis, *Perelandra* (New York: Macmillan, 1944, 1970), 62.

9. Peterson, *Answering God*, 76f.

10. For this section, see E. A. Judge, "St. Paul and Classical Society," *Jahrbuch für Antike und Christentum*, 15, 1972, 21–22, 31; and Helmut Koester, *History, Culture, and Religion of the Hellenistic Age*, Volume One of *Introduction to the New Testament* (Philadelphia: Fortress Press, 1982), 101–13.

11. Hundreds of years later it was still the Greek boast that: "Those who were vanquished by Alexander are happier than those who escaped his hand; for these had no one to put an end to the wretchedness of their existence, while the victor compelled those others to lead a happy life" (Plutarch *Moralia* 328E). In the intertestamental writings, 1 and 2 Maccabees testify to the resentment of Jews at the imposition of the Hellenistic way of life.

12. In both cases, "one" is understood and supplied by the reader.

13. Again, the reader naturally supplies the "one."

14. The reader who knows Greek will see that Revelation 1:4 has another Greek infelicity. The elements of the phrase "who is and who was and who is to come" have become so much a title for Jesus (see 1:8; 4:8; 11:17; 16:5), that John cannot even put the phrase into the genitive case which the preposition that precedes it ("from") demands. It is a problem I do not even know how to reproduce in English, but in Greek it is a clunker.

15. Joseph A Fitzmyer, *The Gospel According to Luke, I–IX* (New York: Doubleday, 1983), 92.

16. In normal literary Greek, this phrase would have been constructed: "And in those days the going out of a decree . . . came to pass." See the discussion about Luke's variation of style in Maximilian Zerwick, S.J., *Biblical Greek Illustrated by Examples*, English edition adapted from the fourth Latin edition by Joseph Smith, S.J. (Rome: *Scripta Potificii Instituti Biblici*, 1963), No. 389 n. 134.

17. Intriguingly, the two times Luke does so he is reproducing sayings from Jesus and Paul (Acts 17:28; 26:14).

18. Moulton and Milligan suggest the term *skubalon* is of vulgar coinage, from the phrase, "to throw to the dogs" (*es kunas balein*), in *Vocabulary of the Greek New Testament Illustrated from the Papyri and Other Non-Literary Sources* (Grand Rapids: Eerdmans, 1980, reprint of the 1st edition of 1930), 579.

19. In conversation with Pierre Babin, as reported in Babin's *The New Era in Religious Communication* (Minneapolis: Fortress Press, 1991), 6.

20. Richard Baxter, *The Saints' Everlasting Rest* 1.4.9: "Reader, stop here, and think awhile what a state this is. Is it a small thing in thine eyes to be beloved of God; to be the son, the spouse, the love, the delight of the King of glory? Christian, believe this, and think on it; thou shalt be eternally embraced in the arms of that love which was from everlasting, and will extend to everlasting: of that love, which brought the Son of God's love from heaven to earth, from earth to the cross, from the cross to the grave, from the grave to glory: that love which was weary, hungry, tempted, scorned, scourged, buffeted, spit upon, crucified, pierced; which did fast, pray, teach, heal, weep, sweat, bleed, die: that love will eternally embrace them. When perfect, created love, and most perfect, uncreated love meet together, oh the blessed meeting!"

21. *Institutes* 4.12.30. Worship leader Barry Liesch offers sound pastoral wisdom from Peter's lesson about all things being clean and Paul's teaching on caring about the weaker brother (*The New Worship* [Grand Rapids: Baker, 1996], chapter 12 [on Acts 10 and 11] and chapter 13 [on Romans 14 and 1 Corinthians 10]).

22. John Frame, *Contemporary Worship Music: A Biblical Defense* (Phillipsburg, NJ: Presbyterian P & R Publishing, 1997), especially 30–42.

23. See Bayles, *Hole in Our Soul*. In surveying the history of American popular music, Bayles has a keen eye for the contribution of African American music to twentieth-century mainstream popular culture.

24. John Piper, "Preaching as Worship: Meditations on Expository Exultation," *Trinity Journal* 16NS (1995), 29–45.

25. See Russell M. Yee, "Shared Meaning and Significance in Congregational Singing," *The Hymn: A Journal of Congregational Song* 42.2 April 1997, 7–11. Psalms and hymns are more stand alone entities, praise songs are more satisfying in juxtaposition. It is less the individual songs that matter but the flow that sets side by side different elements of worship. There may often be a richness to a set of songs that is greater than the sum of its parts—the songs cannot be evaluated, much less appreciated, atomistically. I am reminded of the way Psalm 108 uses portions of previous psalms (Psalm 57 is an individual complaint that ends with trust; and Psalm 60 is a corporate complaint that ends with assurance) to say something new: Psalm 108 weds the confidence sections from both psalms

and "produces a particularly powerful message of conviction in the midst of conflict" (*Spirit of the Reformation Study Bible*, 924).

26. Syncopation is the stressing of a normally weak beat in a measure of music. A back beat is a steady accent on the second and fourth beats of a composition in four-beat measure.

Coda

1. For texts, see Rendell Harris and Alphonse Mingana, *The Odes and Psalms of Solomon* Vol. II: *The Translation* (Manchester: at the University Press, 1920); and James Hamilton Charlesworth, *The Odes of Solomon: The Syriac Texts* (Missoula, MT: Scholars Press, 1977). I find attractive Harris's hypothesis that the *Odes* emanated from Ignatius's Antioch, 43–49, 67–68. On the basis of their parallels with the Qumran scrolls and the Johannine literature, Charlesworth thinks the *Odes*' most probable date is close to AD 100 and not later than 125 and that their affinities with Ignatius support the hypothesis that they were composed within or not far from Antioch (*Critical Reflections on the Odes of Solomon*, Vol. 1: *Literary Setting, Textual Studies, Gnosticism, the Dead Sea Scrolls and the Gospel of John* [Sheffield, England: Sheffield Academic Press, 1998], 23).

2. Ignatius, *Epistle to the Ephesians* 4.1—translation mine.

3. Edmund P. Clowney, *Eutychus (and his Kin)* (Grand Rapids: Eerdmans, 1960). Following are examples of his hymn texts, as they appear in the 1990 edition of the *Trinity Hymnal*: "Vast the Immensity, Mirror of Majesty," no. 24; "We Lift Up as Our Shield God's Name," no. 104, an adaptation of the prayer of St. Patrick of Ireland; "Who Shall Ascend the Mountain of the Lord," no. 292, a christological interpretation of Psalm 24, a text I prefer to sing to the tune *Sine Nomine* by Ralph Vaughan Williams (available for download at <http://www .reggiekidd.com/>); "In Your Arms, Lord Jesus", no. 419; "You Came to Us, Dear Jesus," no. 596, a christological interpretation of the parable of the Good Samaritan; "O Lord, I Love You, My Shield, My Tower," no. 620, a christological interpretation of Psalm 18; "Loved with Everlasting Love," no. 703, an adaptation of George W. Robinson's 1890 hymn by the same title.

4. This, along with many other tributes to Professor Clowney, can be found at www.edmundclowney.com.

5. Clowney, "The Singing Savior," *Moody Monthly* (July-August, 1979), 40–42.

6. Clowney, "The Singing Christ," circa 1980, unpublished; adapted and set to meter by Wade Williams and Reggie Kidd, 2000. Music by Wade Williams and Reggie Kidd, available for download at <http://www.reggiekidd.com/>.

Subject Index

abandonment, 93
Abrahamic covenant, 79
Absalom, 52, 61–62
Ackroyd, Dan, 131
acrostics, 34
Adam, 104–5
aesthetics, 125, 128, 196n9
affect, 175
affections, 31
African American music, 155,
   203n23
Alexander the Great, 168–69, 202n11
already/not yet, 101, 121
Altrogge, Mark, 95
Alzheimer's disease, 87–88, 98
"Amazing Grace," 167
Ambrose, 17, 139, 140
Amnon, 61
ancient-future faith, 155
Anderson, Yohann, 199n5
Andre 3000, 120
Anglo-Catholic worship, 155
Antioch, 204n1
antiphonal singing, 68
Apollos, 138, 140
Apostles' Creed, 156

Aquinas, 142, 198n24
Aristotle, 142, 166, 168, 198n24
ark of the covenant, 64–65, 68
art music, 151
Asaph, 65–67, 190n11
Ashley, Eric, 94
assembly, 125
Augustine, 139, 140
aural architecture, 68–69, 83

Baal, 16
Babin, Pierre, 203n19
Babylonian captivity, 29, 52, 53–54,
   63–64
Bach, Johann Sebastian, 24, 94,
   130, 131, 134–36, 139–40, 150,
   151–52, 199n9
"Bach" voice, 130, 141–42, 172, 179
back beat, 176, 204n26
baptism, 195n13
Baptist hymns, 155
Barnabas, 128
Barrows, Cliff, 18
Bathsheba, 52, 59
Baxter, Richard, 174, 203n20
Bayles, Martha, 162, 203n23

Scripture Index

213

214

Reggie Kidd (Ph. D., Duke University) is professor of New Testament at Reformed Theological Seminary in Orlando. He also is the pastor of worship at Orangewood Presbyterian Church in Maitland, Florida, and serves as a faculty member for the Institute of Worship Studies. When not playing guitar, reading fine books, taking cuts at the batting cage, or cutting bamboo with his samurai sword, he enjoys blogging at www.reggiekidd.com.

CPSIA information can be obtained
at www.ICGtesting.com
Printed in the USA
LVHW040433140123
737123LV00006B/711